almanac

association for welsh writing in english

PARTHIAN

almanac

a yearbook

of

welsh writing

in english

critical
essays

edited by Katie Gramich

association for welsh writing
in english

PARTHIAN

almanac – a yearbook of welsh writing in english: critical essays is supported by the Association for Welsh Writing in English

and is published by
Parthian
The Old Surgery
Napier Street
Cardigan
SA43 1ED
www.parthianbooks.co.uk

First published in 2011

ISBN 978-19069-984-31

The publisher acknowledges the financial
support of the Welsh Books Council.

Printed and bound by Gwasg Gomer, Llandysul, Wales

British Library Cataloguing in Publication Data

A cataloguing record for this book is available from the British Library.

almanac

a yearbook of welsh writing in english: critical essays

vol 15 | 2010–11

Contents:

Welsh Nationalist Horror

Darryl Jones
Trinity College, Dublin

In the last stanza of one of his last poems, 'The Statues', written on April 9, 1938, W. B. Yeats writes:

> When Pearse summoned Cuchulain to his side
> What stalked through the Post Office? What intellect,
> What calculation, number, measurement, replied?
> We Irish, born into that ancient sect
> But thrown upon this filthy modern side
> And by its formless spawning fury wrecked,
> Climb to our proper dark, that we may trace
> The lineaments of a plummet-measured face.[1]

Here, Yeats images the nationalist moment as an *occult* moment, with Patrick Pearse as a bardic geomancer summoning up a mythic terror to the aid of his 'ancient sect', and in doing so also measuring out the land, which is saturated with magic, along a system of ley-lines. Considering his lifelong interest in the occult, given symbolic display as a high-profile member of the Hermetic Order of the Golden Dawn, this, I would suggest, is precisely how one might expect Yeats to render the struggle for Irish independence. While it may be problematic for contemporary nationalists in these islands, the interpenetration of their own ideology with the discourse of occultism remains an uncomfortable fact, and one which continues to resurface, particularly in popular cultural forms, since popular culture is modernity's classic medium for the displaced or symbolic articulation of contemporary anxieties. Horror, most particularly of all, presents narratives of violence, often unsystematic, chaotic, or contradictory, but nevertheless operating in response to specific sets of cultural-political concerns, a distorted mirror which enables a glimpse of things as they are. Realism is an ideologically-centralising, or even an epistemologically-imperialist form, presupposing a cultural and political stability commensurate with the 'knowable communities' which its narratives present. Modern Wales, riven by geographical, linguistic, cultural and class divides, has offered no such certainties.[2]

The 1960s and 70s was a galvanising period for Welsh nationalist thinking and activism. Rereading two of the key texts of modern nationalism, both produced in this period, Saunders Lewis's 'Tynged yr Iaith' ('The Fate of the Language', 1962) and Ned Thomas's *The Welsh Extremist* (1971), gives a real sense of the urgency of the times, rendered in language which verges, for understandable reasons, on the apocalyptic.[3] As is well known, Cymdeithas yr Iaith Gymraeg (The Welsh Language Society), committed to activism and civil disobedience, was founded in 1962, in response to the call of 'Tynged yr Iaith'. Small-scale physical-force nationalist groups also came into being in this period.[4] Mudiad Amddiffyn Cymru (MAC, Movement for the Defence of Wales) was formed in 1963, in response to the plans to flood the Tryweryn valley and the village of Capel Celyn in order to provide water for Liverpool (the valley was drowned in 1965); they also bombed the Clywedog dam and a water-supply from Lake Vyrnwy, two more reservoirs built from drowned valleys. The paramilitary Free Wales Army, led by Julian Cayo Evans, dates from 1965, though its actions seem to have been confined to spectacle rather than sabotage. The activities of Mudiad Amddiffyn Cymru, reconfiguring themselves as 'MAC 2', gained a new focus at the time of the investiture of the Prince of Wales in Caernarfon Castle on 1 July, 1969. On 30 June, two activists, George Taylor and Alwyn Jones were blown up in Abergele whilst assembling a bomb near a railway line along which the Royal train was due to pass on its way to the investiture. No one knows precisely what their intentions were. The investiture took place on the same day as the sentencing of three members of the Free Wales Army, including Cayo Evans, on firearms and explosives charges, a coincidence which proved irresistibly symbolic for many nationalists.[5]

Mudiad Amddiffyn Cymru was not driven by any particular creed or ideology. Unlike the intellectually-sophisticated middle-class cultural nationalists who tended to comprise the membership of Plaid Cymru in the 1960s, MAC's membership was largely working class, both Anglophone and Welsh-speaking, and drawn from both North and South Wales (its founder, Owen Williams, was a Welsh-speaking farmer from Llŷn its director of operations, John Jenkins, an Anglophone Newport soldier). These men were driven to violence by an inchoate sense of oppression and colonial anxiety, an unbearable sense that their culture was under threat, or that they were not at home in their own country. As John Humphries writes, 'these activists were essentially fundamentalists resisting further assimilation through direct action. Sometimes, unable to articulate their enmity and frustration beyond the bar-room door, they turned to violence because they saw no other way to pursue their legitimate grievances.'[6]

The constitutional nationalists of Plaid Cymru, and particularly its leader, the pacifist Gwynfor Evans, were openly condemnatory of political violence, whatever the cause, though many Welsh intellectuals were, if not supportive, then at least highly sympathetic towards the aims of the Abergele bombers. Bobi Jones wrote that 'Everyone who has in the least assisted in the psychological and material subjection of Wales is responsible for their deaths', while Ned Thomas asserted that 'I should find it impossible to hand over to the police a Welsh bomb-layer'.[7] Trefor Beasley, the Llangennech language activist whose campaign in the early 1960s for bilingual rates notices from Llanelli Rural District Council had partly inspired Lewis's 'Tynged yr Iaith', had, according to Humphries, close associations with MAC 2, as did the poet and editor Harri Webb.[8]

Unsurprisingly, it was Saunders Lewis, the foremost nationalist ideologue and activist, who was to be most unwavering in his support of nationalist violence. By the 1960s, Lewis had become estranged from the leadership of Plaid Cymru, largely over their refusal to act decisively and unconstitutionally to prevent the drowning of Tryweryn, which he described as 'a gross and degrading betrayal of all that the Party was established to defend'; Plaid, he believed, had become 'a nest of Aldermaston Anglo-Welsh socialists, and I loathe them'.[9] As early as 1963, in response to MAC's first acts of sabotage in Tryweryn, Lewis wrote to Kate Roberts, 'Gyda'r bechgyn sy'n torri'r gyfraith ac yn wynebu ar garchar y mae fy holl gydymdeimlad i, ac ynddynt hwy a'u dilynwyr yn unig y mae gobaith' ['All of my sympathies are with the boys who break the law and face prison, and only in them and their followers is there hope'].[10] While he was scornful of the phoney militarism of the Free Wales Army, he nevertheless understood their imprisonment as an act of calculated colonial oppression. They were political prisoners:

> Eu carcharu yn wystlon a wnaed, yn wystlon dros unrhyw genedlaetholwyr a wrthwynebai mewn unrhyw fodd yr arwisgo yng Nghaernarfon.... Gwystlon drosom ni, bob un ohonom, ni sy'n ffieiddio'r arwisgiad ac yn awchus am ddisodli llywodraeth Seisnig ar Gymru. Trosom ni y bu eu poen, trosom ni y mae eu carchar.
> [They were imprisoned as hostages, as hostages for any nationalist who opposed the investiture in Caernarfon in any way.... Hostages for us, every one of us, we who execrate the investiture and are eager to overthrow English government in Wales. Their pain is for us, their imprisonment is for us.][11]

In 1968, in a televised interview with Meirion Edwards,

Lewis made his fullest public pronouncements about the justice of spilling Welsh blood in the nationalist cause: I shall return to this interview at the end of the article.

Constitutional nationalism, meanwhile, poured its energies in the 1970s into the devolution campaign. The shambles of the devolution referendum in 1979, conducted under conditions which made a Yes vote practically impossible (it required the mandate of 40% of the electorate), and in the teeth of a viciously hostile No campaign spearheaded by Welsh Labour MPs such as Neil Kinnock, led directly to a resurgence in nationalist violence. Meibion Glyn Dŵr commenced their campaign of firebombing English-owned second homes in December 1979 (and it is worth noting in passing that 'Meibion Glyn Dŵr' can plausibly be translated not only as the Sons of Owain Glyndwr but as 'Sons of the Drowned Valley').

Given the links I posited earlier between cultural anxiety, on the one hand, and popular cultural production on the other, one would expect to find many works of horror dating from the 1960s and after to be concerned, explicitly or obliquely, with the ideas and anxieties raised by these nationalist concerns, and particularly with exploring the relationship between nationalism and violence. Furthermore, rather in the manner of Yeats or of Arthur Machen, one would expect them to be powerfully inflected by the overlapping discourses of Celticism and occultism, both of which, for reasons paralleling the proliferation of nationalist activities, were resurgent in popular culture throughout the 1960s and 70s. And we do find many such examples, though not necessarily originating in Wales. It is one part of my argument here that these are ideas and anxieties which cannot and should not be contained within Offa's Dyke, but which have implications for a broader archipelagic identity politics. My Wales here has a permeable border, and one which will often move us some way outside the traditionally understood confines of the nation. Borders are, after all, unstable markers or boundaries of identity, both geopolitically and psychologically, and they are also, as interstitial spaces, the classic sites for the production of anxiety, fear, or abjection. My border, in other words, is geomantic rather than geopolitical.

My first example, then, is not Welsh at all, but does provide an influential paradigm for the modes of ideological representation to be found in works of Welsh nationalist horror. By far the most celebrated work of Celtic horror produced in this period is Robin Hardy's classic 1973 film *The Wicker Man*, in which police sergeant Neil Howie from the Scottish mainland investigates the disappearance of a child on the remote island of Summerisle, and finds his own Christianity confronted and counteracted by the Pagan beliefs of the Summerislanders. At the film's celebrated close, the islanders ritualistically sacrifice him as a burnt offering inside a giant Wicker Man, in order to ensure the ripeness of their apple harvest.

The Summerislanders are certainly separatists, but are they to be understood as nationalists? The film's screenplay was written by Anthony Shaffer, and is far more influenced by his recent reading of J. G. Frazer's monumental work of comparative mythography, *The Golden Bough*, than by any recent developments in Celtic nationalist ideology, of which the film seems completely unconscious. In a recent article in *Sight and Sound*, Rob Lewis has included *The Wicker Man* as an example of a resurgence in British rural cinema in the late 60s and 70s, placing it alongside that other cult classic, Michael Reeves's *Witchfinder General*, as part of a tendency which Lewis understands as fundamentally *English* (and both Hardy and Shaffer were themselves English).[12] Nevertheless, the film does deal in themes and ideas commonly associated with both nationalist and anti-nationalist discourse (and the two really do collapse into one another throughout): ruralism, occultism, anti-industrialism, anti-modernity, Celticism, violence, blood sacrifice. (The image of the Wicker Man itself derives from Julius Caesar's *Commentary on the Gallic Wars*, wherein he records the sacrificial rites of the Druids of Gaul, burning human offerings inside giant wicker men.)

The politics of casting form an important component of any cult film – it means something to cast certain actors in certain roles. *The Wicker Man* has one of the most *outré* casts ever assembled for a film, in which there are famously no Scottish actors in any of the leading roles: Sergeant Howie is played by the English actor Edward Woodward; Lord Summerisle by the Anglo-Italian actor Christopher Lee; local sexpot Willow McGregor by Swedish sexpot Britt Ekland; Miss Rose the schoolteacher by the Australian Diane Cilento; the librarian by the Polish Ingrid Pitt; and the landlord Alder McGregor (Willow's father) by the English dancer and mime Lindsay Kemp. The film's notably folky, Celtic soundtrack, is by the Italian-American musician Paul Giovanni.[13] What is going on here? Some readers may be reminded of John Ford's *How Green Was My Valley* (1941), and particularly of that film as refracted through the lens of Christopher Meredith's 1988 novel, *Shifts*, where it is the subject of a celebrated diatribe by one of the main characters, protesting that the film offers a Gilfach Goch which somehow contains only one actual Welsh person, Rhys Davies (who plays Dai Bando the pugilist). I have written elsewhere about the Welsh village of Llanwelly, formerly Llansileffraillerychmair, in George Waggner's *The Wolf Ma*n (1941), populated by Americans, English, Hungarians and Russians, but with no actual Welsh people at all. Superficially, then, this is a matter of the cavalier disregard of a cultural-imperialist film industry for local national sensitivities and indigenous cultures.[14] But there are other possibilities. *The Wicker Man's* casting troubles monolithic notions of national identity, as well as adding a genuine element of uncanny disorientation to the film. More than this, I want to remind readers of Freud's hypothesis in *Moses and Monotheism* (his last major work, written in 1938, around the same time that Yeats was composing 'The Statues') that the greatest of all Old Testament prophets and patriarchs was not in fact Jewish at all: 'Moses, the liberator and law-giver of the Jewish people, was not a Jew but an Egyptian'.[15] Moses, in other words, is to be understood as a necessary outsider. This, I suggest, has profound implications for the psycho-politics of nationalist thinking.[16] Nationalist leaders and icons need not be and perhaps *should not be* members of the indigenous national group, but rather displaced, at one remove, liminal, capable of being extruded or abjected from the nation when their work is done; classic scapegoats, sacrificial victims. This is an argument which I shall be silently activating at various points throughout the rest of this article.

Filmed by HTV across the long, hot summer of 1976 in the village of Avebury, Wiltshire, *Children of the Stones* is often referred to as '*The Wicker Man* for children': the inhabitants of the village are devotees of a pagan star-cult, under the leadership of the sinister local squire, played by the terrifying Scottish actor Iain Cuthbertson, who features alongside the Welsh actor Gareth Thomas, and Freddie Jones, born in Stoke-on-Trent but here playing a displaced Welsh miner, Dai. Avebury, some 40 miles from the Welsh border, is a village completely enclosed within a circle of Neolithic standing stones, which *Children of the Stones* situates as an *omphalos* at the centre of a radiating fan of ley-lines.

Standing stones are a recurring feature of nationalist horror, as they were in the poetic symbology of Yeats, who had read the following hypothesis in Ernest Renan's essay 'La Poésie des Races Celtiques':

> The stone, in truth, seems the natural symbol of the Celtic races. It is an immutable witness that has no death. The animal, the plant, above all the human figure, only express the divine life under a determinate form; the stone on the

> contrary, adapted to receive all forms, has been the fetish of peoples in their childhood.... The *men-hir* to be met with over the whole surface of the ancient world, what is it but a monument of primitive humanity, a living witness to its faith in heaven.[17]

Like Renan, Yeats came to believe that the ancient Celts worshipped stones: as he wrote, gnomically, in his most celebrated political poem, 'Easter 1916':

> Hearts with one purpose alone
> Through summer and winter seem
> Enchanted to a stone
> To trouble the living stream ...
> Minute by minute they live:
> The stone's in the midst of all.[18]

The theory of the existence of ley-lines, pre-Christian 'trackways' or lines of force along which mystical sights are aligned, is a body of occult thinking profoundly associated with the Welsh border, having first been theorised by the Hereford archaeologist Alfred Watkins in his book *The Old Straight Track: Its Mounds, Beacons, Moats, Sites and Mark-Stones* (1925). (He named them 'ley-lines' after the suffix '-ley', meaning 'clearing', which occurs in many place-names situated along these lines.) Watkins did the great majority of his research for this work on the Welsh border, and uses the Vale of Radnor, in particular, and the Black Mountains as test-cases for his theory that the landscape is criss-crossed by hundreds of Neolithic paths, marked out by 'ley-men', originally as straight routes to the location of salt, flint, clay, or other important commodities for hunter-gatherers. Stones are crucial to Watkins's alignment of leys, as markers along the roads, or as places of ceremonial ritual (often situated where leys begin, or cross one another). These ritual stones (stone circles, cromlechs, dolmens) were often altar-stones, places of sacrifice aligned to the midsummer sun. The druids, who supervised these stones, derived their authority, Watkins believed, from their ley-men predecessors: 'ley-man, astronomer-priest, druid, bard, wizard, witch, palmer, and hermit, were all more or less linked by one thread of ancient knowledge and power'.[19] While the book was to become influential for later esoteric thinking, Watkins is careful throughout *The Old Straight Track* not to make occult speculations about the ley-lines (although others, developing his work, certainly did); and although the work does bear the impress of *The Golden Bough*, Watkins does not really discuss the origins of the ley-lines and their stones in heliolatry and its rites, nor their connections with human sacrifice, except as an unprovable inference to be drawn from his system. His primary objective is to demonstrate that the ley-lines exist, not to offer conjectures as to why they might exist. Nevertheless, Watkins does concede that ritual and magic did come to form an important component of the ley-lines: 'Utility was the primary object. Later on, magic, religion and superstition blended with the system'.[20] Many of Watkins's readers, however, were not so scrupulous in their distinctions.

First published in 1970, in the wake of the direct action campaigns, *Y Gromlech yn yr Haidd* (*The Cromlech in the Barley*) is a nationalist parable by the novelist and Plaid Cymru candidate Islwyn Ffowc Elis, in which the removal of standing stones signifies violent colonial oppression, standing in metaphorically for the drowning of valleys, and precipitates occult vengeance. Elis was born in Dyffryn Ceiriog, within sight of the English border, in 1924, a year after the valley had narrowly escaped being drowned to provide water for Warrington. As Elis was later to testify, the psycho-geography of his liminal, border-country upbringing profoundly informed his nationalist sensibilities:

Nid ar lechweddau Arfon y magwyd fi, lle na chlywid

> Saesneg ond ar antur chwarter canrif yn ôl, ond dwy filltir a hanner o ffin Loegr, lle'r oedd pob cyfathrach â'r tu allan i'r dyffryn cul, Cymraeg yn golygu Saesneg. Dyna, rwy'n meddwl, pam yr aeth 'brwydr yr iaith' i graidd fy modd ac felly'n amod i'm hysgrifennu.... Fe ffurfiwyd pob llenor yn ystod deng mlynedd cynta'i oes, ac ni allaf newid fy neng mlynedd cyntaf. Y mae'r ffin yn fy ngwaed.
> [I was not raised on the slopes of Arfon, where English was never heard except by chance until a quarter of a century ago, but two and a half miles from the English border, where every intercourse outside of the narrow, Welsh valley meant English. That, I think, is why the 'battle for the language' went to the core of my being and so became a condition of my writing. Every writer is formed in the first ten years of his life, and I can't change my first ten years. The border is in my blood.][21]

In *Y Gromlech yn yr Haidd*, Bill Henderson, an English incomer to a North Wales farm, who comes with 'chwant meistrolgar am foderneiddio popeth o fewn cyrraedd ... beiriant o ddyn sy'n tynnu hanes i fyny o'r gwraidd' ('a masterly desire to modernise everything within reach ... a man-machine who pulls history up by the roots'), hubristically attempts to remove three standing stones – 'arswydus o hen. yr neb pa mor hen' ('terrifyingly old. No one knows how old') – from the middle of his barley-field, in spite of warnings that they should not be touched, that they are a Neolithic burial site.[22] The scene is set for a clash between indigenous, pre-modern, pagan Welsh traditions, and secular, colonialising English techno-modernity: 'Does gen *i* ddim amser i hen ofergoelion dwl. Carreg ydy carreg. Dyna i gyd. Dim ond carreg.' ('I have no time for stupid old superstitions. A stone is a stone. That's all. Just a stone'). Henderson belongs to a 'pitiful race' ('hiliogaeth druenus') of rootless English exiles: 'Wyddon nhw ddim beth ydy sefyll, ac ymlonyddu, mewn un goleuni sefydlog' ('They do not know how to stay, how to remain still, in one constant light').[23] The removal of the first stone coincides with Henderson's wife miscarrying. The removal of the second precipitates an outbreak of foot-and-mouth disease, which Henderson brings back with him from a visit to Gloucestershire (the implication is obvious: the English are a plague). With the removal of the third stone, Henderson is attacked by invisible supernatural creatures, and temporarily loses his identity, which is subsumed into that of 'Kia', a Neolithic hunter-gatherer. At the close of the novel he is a broken man.

In counterpoint to Henderson's colonial English modernity, Benni Rees, the 'local encyclopedia' and self-confessed pagan, appeals to an older law when Constable Jenkins tells him that Henderson is on the right side of the law: 'I'ch cyfraith *chi*, ydy.... Ond mae 'na gyfraith arall' ('*Your* law, yes ... But there is another law').[24] The appeal to a higher law, transcending colonial law, is the classic strategy of nationalist civil disobedience and, as a Plaid Cymru activist, it seems likely that Elis is alluding directly here to the defence made by Saunders Lewis in his speech from the dock in Caernarfon Court, on 13 October 1936, when on trial for the Penyberth arson, the paradigmatic moment of Welsh nationalist direct action:

> On the other hand, if you find us not guilty you declare your conviction as judges in this matter that the moral law is supreme; you declare that the moral law is binding on governments just as it is on private citizens. You declare that 'necessity of state' gives no right to set morality aside, and you declare that justice, not material force, must rule in the affairs of nations.
>
> We hold with unshakeable conviction that the burning of the monstrous bombing range in Lleyn was an act forced on us for the defence of Welsh civilization, for the defence of Christian principles, for the maintenance of the Law of God in Wales. Nothing else was possible for us. It was the Government itself that created the situation in which we

> were placed, so that we had to choose either the way of cowards, and slink out of the defence of Christian tradition and morality, or we had to act as we acted, and trust to a jury of our countrymen to declare that the Law of God is superior to every other law, and that by that law our act is just.[25]

It is a version of this defence which animates all the direct-action nationalism with which this essay is concerned.

The Newport director Julian Richards's film *Darklands* (1996) is an unambiguous attempt to render a Welsh *Wicker Man*, and with unambiguously political resonances, as Port Talbot journalist Frazer Truick (the very cockney Craig Fairbrass) investigates the disappearance of a local steelworker against a background of post-industrial recession and unemployment, and finds himself the victim of a sacrificial Druidic cult led by the local Plaid Cymru MP, David Keller (played by the Surrey-born Jon Finch). Richards clearly understands his film as operating in a political context, saying in a 2004 interview:

> On the one hand Darklands is a film that uses cultural, political, social and economic issues in Wales to serve its agenda as a generic horror film dealing with conspiracy and paranoia. It's not meant to be an accurate, realistic portrayal of life in Wales or of Welsh nationalism, but more a piece of fantasy or metaphor that draws upon and exaggerates real ingredients to create a mythology. But where there is smoke there is fire and I think the subtext of Darklands is ultimately about Celtic cultural angst, depicted in a conflict between the happy to be anglicised Welsh and the nationalists.[26]

Read as a realist text, *Darklands* makes no sense at all, but this may only be to say that it contains the ostensible contradictions and paradoxes which seem characteristic of nationalist horror. As many readers will already have found themselves thinking, the chance of Port Talbot's having returned a Plaid Cymru MP in the 1990s was frankly slim, though one can but hope. Even more implausible is that that MP should be played by Jon Finch, with a Welsh accent that could best be described as 'optimistic'. David Keller's father, Emyr, was a notable Welsh mythographer, we are told, a kind of homegrown J. G. Frazer, and author of the seminal study *Arwydd Paganaidd* ('The Pagan Sign'). Keller is first seen preaching 'a cultural reawakening', and later admonishes Truick for not having learned his native tongue, in spite of the fact that he himself, on the evidence we have here, clearly does not speak Welsh (he twice tries, and fails, to pronounce *Arwydd Paganaidd*). Truick was brought up in London but returns to his native Port Talbot, where he is sacrificed at the close of the film by the nationalist pagans (including the late Welsh cultural icon Ray Gravell as a blowtorch-wielding heavy), his throat cut as he hangs inside the steelworks, to propitiate the gods in order to end recession and unemployment. In its crude way, the film does give articulation to real anxieties about the devastation of industrial South Wales under Thatcherism, and ends with a full-blooded mystico-nationalist chant spoken and sung in the Celtic style by Heather Jones:

> Cyflawnwn iti'r baban hwn, Meseia i'r wlad wastraff hon. Tywalltir ei waed i'th ddiwallu. Fe'th fwydir gan ei gnawd. Rho i'm fywyd, ni ofynwn fwy.
> [We present to you this baby, a Messiah for this waste land. His blood is spilled to replenish you. You are fed by his flesh. Give us life, we ask no more.]

In the early 1990s, the Lancashire-born writer (and BBC Radio Wales presenter) Phil Rickman began to publish what became a series of occult novels, mostly set on the Welsh border. His first novel, *Candlenight* (1991) is set in the fictional Cardiganshire village of 'Y Groes', and has its origins in *Aliens*, a 1987 radio documentary which Rickman made about English incomers to Wales. *Candlenight* offers an extended exploration of the relationship between nationalism and occultism, and is one of a number of works from the 1990s which provide a popular-cultural rendering of the activities of Meibion Glyn Dŵr and other ultra-nationalist organizations. In *Candlenight*, a series of English incomers are bloodily dispatched by the natives, guardians of the body of Owain Glyn Dŵr himself, whose return to revitalise the nation is presaged at the novel's end when nationalist historian Guto Evans encounters a spectral figure in a blizzard on the night of the by-election in which he is standing as a Plaid Cymru candidate.

Candlenight clearly counterpoints the constitutional nationalism of Plaid Cymru, to which it is extremely sympathetic, with ultra-nationalist separatism, which has its origins in Druidic paganism: like *The Wicker Man*'s Summerisle, or *Darklands*' Port Talbot, Y Groes – an idyllic, organic community made up entirely of Welsh-speakers – replenishes itself though human sacrifice, demanding the blood of its English enemies:

> 'The old Druids, see,' Aled said. 'They did not sacrifice each other, their – you know, virgins, kids. None of that nonsense.'
> History lessons, Berry thought, Wales is all about history lessons.
> 'But I've heard it said they used to sacrifice their enemies,' Aled said. 'Their prisoners. A life's a life, see, isn't it? Blood is blood.'[27]

The community's spiritual leader is the Reverend Elias ap Siencyn, a 'loony Welsh Nationalist vicar' (in the words of one character), clearly a caricature of R. S. Thomas, whose own views on nationalist direct action became increasingly outspoken during the 1980s, but also with a sly nod at the

Reverend Eli Jenkins, spiritual leader of that other idyllic Welsh village, Dylan Thomas's Llareggub.[28]

While Guto Evans is certainly a member of Cymdeithas yr Iaith Gymraeg, and hints at a MAC-style background (his car had at one point been fitted with a concealed police tracking-device), the inhabitants of Y Groes are uninterested in constitutional politics (they do not turn up to an election meeting called in the village hall). Guto is not a fundamentalist ideologue but a second-language Welsh speaker from the South Wales valleys, and the author of a revisionist history of Glyn Dŵr which presents the Welsh leader as a proto-socialist. Bethan, the local village schoolteacher (a widow, whose English husband was sacrificed to the village), explains gradations of nationalism to the American journalist Morelli:

> 'You see ... there are different kinds of Welsh nationalism. There is Plaid Cymru, which envisages a self-governing Wales with its own economic structure – an independent, bilingual state within the European Community. And there is another sort, which you might compare with the National Front, the Ku Klux Klan, yes?'
>
> 'Extreme right wing.'
>
> 'Except they would not think of themselves like that. They are protecting their heritage, they feel the same things we all feel from time to time, but –' She sighed again. 'I'm afraid there are some people for whom being Welsh is more important than being human.'
>
> 'And – let me guess here – this type of person sees Plaid as a half-baked outfit which no longer represents the views of the real old Welsh nation, right?'[29]

Morelli and Bethan become lovers, an expository narrative device which enables the novel to explain its political concerns to a non-nationalist (in fact, a non-Welsh) implied readership. When Morelli expresses his belief that Wales is 'just about the most obscure country in Western

Europe', and that nationalism is 'an outdated concept', Bethan gives him a lesson in recent nationalist history:

> 'How else can we defend what is ours? The English wanted more water for Liverpool and Birmingham, so they came into Wales and flooded our valleys. Whole Welsh villages at the bottom of English reservoirs.... I know, that was years ago. But they are doing it again. Only this time they're flooding us with people and they're drowning our language and our culture.'[30]

The novel's ideological stance (or perhaps its political unconscious, if 'ideological stance' is too overt) is allied with constitutional nationalism within Westminster, rather than with the fringe activities of direct-action groups, which it figures as a locus of horror: the incomers and the constitutional nationalists are afforded narrative agency, space, and readerly sympathy, in ways that the extremists are not. The latter are rendered as terrifying physical and moral grotesques, inhabitants of a Wales consistently imaged in terms of the past and the supernatural.

Rickman's follow-up to *Candlenight* was *Crybbe* (1993), an enormous work of border horror set in a town (a fictional amalgam of Knighton and Presteigne) which straddles the English-Welsh border, but whose name derives from the Welsh *crybachu*, 'to wither'. *Crybbe* deploys the full panoply of occultist beliefs, from stone circles (like Avebury, Crybbe is completely enclosed within standing stones) and ley-lines to spirit-healing, tarot and regression, and is heavily influenced by John Cowper Powys's *A Glastonbury Romance* (1932), just as *Candlenight* bears some of the impress of Powys's *Owen Glendower* (1940). Powys was of course himself an esoteric, liminal Welsh writer – and one of *Crybbe's* main characters is a Hereford-based occult writer named J. M. Powys, purportedly a direct descendent of John Cowper, and author of *The Old Golden Land*, a new-age classic.

Crybbe quotes the following passage from *The Old Golden Land*:

> The border country – any border country – has a special quality. Two cultures merging, two types of landscape, an atmosphere of change and uncertainty. In such places, it used to be said, the veil between this world and others is especially thin. Border country: a transition zone ... a psychic departure lounge.[31]

Some of the same issues recur in more-than-usually outlandish fashion in the pulp novelist Guy N. Smith's *The Knighton Vampires* (also 1993). Here, the Welsh border town of Knighton (Tref-y-Clawdd; 'Dyke Town') suffers from a series of vampire attacks. At the same time, a nationalist splinter group is burning holiday cottages. The man behind it all is Glyn Idle, South Wales property magnate turned Plaid Cymru politician, who has enlisted the aid of a local hippie convoy, camping out at the nearby Cantlin Stone. The vampires are in fact local crack addicts who have been fitted with fanged steel dentures. Idle arranges for a bomb to be planted in Knighton clock tower, timed to explode during a Bank Holiday celebration. The bomb is a dud, inexpertly made, and does not detonate. The crack vampires turn on Idle in an act of cannibalism. The novel closes with news of a bomb exploding in the English Department of Cardiff University.

The opening of the novel sees Knighton in the grip of an 'anti-English campaign', with the graffiti 'ENGLISH GO HOME' spraypainted on town walls.[32] The nonagenarian Sid the Keeper, custodian of the town's folk memory (another 'local encyclopedia'), tells the secret policeman, Mayo:

> 'Now these Welsh loonies are trying to drive out the English. I'm Welsh,' he added, almost apologetically. 'But Knighton's multi-racial, Welsh and English. We mix, no bother. It's

> these activators, or whatever you call them, as is stirring it all up.'[33]

In a manner characteristic of my subject, these nationalist 'activators' are also the hippies, a new-age convoy who have settled nearby, and who exercise a shadowy influence over the novel, frequently discussed but never really seen. They are the occult nationalists who may or may not be vampires, and who come to carry out ancestral, supernatural national vengeance:

> 'Legend, probably [says the Keeper], one o' them that sounded too daft to put in the books. According to Granddad, and my memory's as sharp as it was when he told me, those English-Welsh wars was pretty fierce, a lot got killed. Well, the Welsh dead won't accept defeat, they're lying there in their graves awaiting the call. And when the time comes they'll rise up like that there Dracula chap and drive the English back over the border. Well, we've got the vampires, haven't we, and these anarchists are settin' fire to English-owned buildings. It's like the dead 'ave got up out of their graves and are takin' their revenge hundreds of years after they was killed.'[34]

It would be fair to say that *The Knighton Vampires* is an ideologically-confused novel, raising issues it is simply ill-equipped to address. Like much English pulp horror, from Dennis Wheatley to James Herbert, it is animated by a robust right-wing populism, a set of xenophobic preoccupations barely concealed by the surface of the text. Glyn Idle propounds a constitutional-nationalist position close to that of Gwynfor Evans:

> He abhorred violence, denounced the arsonists, called for a cessation of the graffiti which was 'abhorrent to the Welsh culture and to the environment'. Devolution, he insisted, would be won through the ballot box.[35]

This seems a legitimate position, but Mayo, who kills for the state, and whose position the novel fully endorses, broods over 'those who sought to destroy a democracy under the guise of devolution. Mayo had been trained to regard terrorists as a natural enemy that must be destroyed at all times, at whatever cost'.[36] The novel, in other words, can only understand constitutional nationalism as a threat to the state, and makes no distinctions between Plaid Cymru and Meibion Glyn Dŵr – or indeed between Meibion Glyn Dŵr and Satanism.

It might perhaps be unfair to expect ideological nuance from Smith, a prolific pulp writer whose most celebrated series of novels is about an invasion of giant crabs, beginning with *Night of the Crabs* in 1976, and including such titles as *Crabs on the Rampage, Crabs: The Human Sacrifice*, and the short story 'Crustacean Vengeance', and whose large *oeuvre* also includes *Sexy Secrets of Swinging Wives, Part 1: The Partner Swappers*. Nevertheless, a comparable degree of ideological confusion is found when even very sophisticated writers venture into Border Country, and beyond into Wales itself.

Phil Rickman's third novel, *The Man in the Moss* (1994), is set on the Cheshire-Derbyshire border, in the isolated community of Bridelow, 'a place of pre-Christian worship' surrounded by 'astronomically-oriented' stone circles, and whose church is sited on a 'presumed prehistoric burial mound'. Bridelow is the 'last refuge of the English Celts. A more pure, undiluted strain than you'll find anywhere in Western Europe'. While there's an element of diminishing returns in a formulaic genre-writer like Rickman, one thing about *The Man in the Moss* is worthy of note here, which is that its villain, the occult Derbyshire children's writer John Peveril Stanage, author of *The Bridestones* and tales of 'King Arthur in Manchester', is partly a fictionalised version of the great occult Cheshire children's writer, Alan Garner.[38]

Garner first came to prominence in 1960 when he

published *The Weirdstone of Brisingamen*, a work of ruralist Arthurian Celticism, set, like most of Garner's work, around his beloved Alderley Edge, which is about 30 miles from the Welsh border. Garner's next two novels, *The Moon of Gomrath* (1964) and *Elidor* (1965) both counterpointed postwar Cheshire with a supernatural Celticism (Garner derived *Elidor* from his reading of Gerald of Wales, and *The Weirdstone* and *Gomrath* from *Sir Gawain and the Green Knight*), but in 1967 he crossed over the geographical border to produce a full-scale work of occult nationalism, *The Owl Service*.

The Owl Service is a retelling of the Blodeuwedd myth, from the fourth branch of the *Mabinogi*, 'Math Fab Mathonwy', in which the sorcerer Gwydion weaves a wife from flowers, Blodeuwedd, for his nephew, Lleu Llaw Gyffes. Blodeuwedd plots to kill Lleu with her lover Gronw Bebyr. Lleu has his revenge on Gronw by killing him with a spear which pierces the standing stone behind which Gronw shelters; Gwydion transforms Blodeuwedd into an owl.

Garner was inspired to write *The Owl Service* by his reading of the *Mabinogi*, but also by holidaying in 'a house in a remote valley in North Wales' – the valley itself is unnamed, but is probably Dyffryn Nantlle (or Nant Lleu) in Gwynedd.[39] Written in the midst of the resurgence in direct-action nationalism in the mid-to-late 60s, the novel is shot through with contemporary Welsh nationalist language and concerns in ways which it is unable to assimilate or even fully to understand. Alison and Roger and their family are English incomers to the valley, the owners of the largest house in the neighbourhood. Alison becomes preoccupied with a dinner service which has a mysterious pattern variously seen as flowers or owls, while Roger obsessively photographs a local standing stone which has a smooth hole through its centre. In their employment, as variously domestics and handymen, are a number of Welsh characters, including Huw, a lifelong resident, and Gwyn, a grammar school boy who has returned to the valley with his mother, who moved away to Aberystwyth when Gwyn was a child. The English are landowners who employ the Welsh as their servants; the Welsh reject capitalist modernity in favour of mystical ruralism, 'wizards and blood all over the place'.[40] At one point, when the supernatural order threatens to overwhelm him, Gwyn keeps hold of his sanity by thinking of the Act of Union: '1536, Statute of Union! 1543, Wales divided into twelve counties! Representatives sent to Westminster!'[41] The issues raised in *The Owl Service* are, in fact, precisely those which Ned Thomas was to analyse in the opening chapters of *The Welsh Extremist* four years later. Roger and Gwyn, English and Welsh, are at odds, sometimes violently, throughout the novel, and through their disagreements embody the nationalist debates of 1960s Wales:

> 'Where's everybody gone to?' said Roger. 'Most of the houses in the valley look empty.'
>
> 'Who's going to rent to us when stuffed shirts from Birmingham pay eight quid a week so that they can swank about their cottage in Wales?
>
> 'Would you want to live here?'
>
> 'I ought to be in Parliament,' said Gwyn.

While Gwyn's mother starts 'talk[ing] like a Welsh Nationalist!', Roger can only understand this ideological position in terms of a racist, occult secret society: Alison renders 'Lleu Llaw Gyffes' as 'Clue Claw Somebody', which Roger in turn renders as 'Ku Klux Klan'[42]. Gwyn and Alison discuss the drowning of valleys:

> 'I can see why these valleys make good reservoirs,' said Alison. 'All you have to do is put a dam across the bottom end.'
>
> 'Not the most tactful remark,' said Gwyn. 'But you're dead right'....

> 'I don't think it can be finished,' said Gwyn. 'I think this valley really is a kind of reservoir. The house, look, smack in the middle, with the mountains all round, shutting it in, guarding the house. I think the power is always there and always will be. It builds up and builds up until it has to be let loose – like filling and emptying a dam.'[43]

At the end of the novel, the valley itself is almost drowned in an apocalyptic storm, and for all of its radical Celtic chic, *The Owl Service* closes with real bathos and shocking ideological complicity, as Roger reasserts the rational, capitalist English order upon the novel by a simple act of disbelief in the supernatural, while Gwyn skulks away. In the novel's final struggle, Alison, the most ambiguous character, aligns herself with the English, not the Welsh.

What Alan Garner may not have known is that the Blodeuwedd myth came with a provenance for contemporary Welsh nationalist culture and ideology, as it was the subject of the greatest work by the greatest of all Cheshire writers, Saunders Lewis. Like all of Lewis's works, *Blodeuwedd* articulates his complex intellectual nationalism, with Blodeuwedd herself advocating political violence: 'A fu erioed un wlad/Na farnodd draes o'i lwyddo yn haeddu llwyddo?' ('Was there ever one country/ That did not judge violence, when it had succeeded, as deserving of success?')[44] *Blodeuwedd* was written in stages between 1923 and 1948, and Lewis once joked in 1931 that, if elected to Parliament, he could finish the play while Lloyd George made his speeches. There's a kind of Romantic Fascistic appeal to Blodeuwedd herself – the sublime beauty of terror – to be counterpointed with the tradition-based classicism that Lewis believed was at the heart of Welsh national identity – though it is part of the play's greatness that it does not, as the Welsh national party itself in the 30s and 40s did not, shirk the appeal of Fascism, which may be overwhelming, and is certainly easier to understand (and to present as a political platform) than the remote austerity of Lewis's Modernistic Tradition.

In a BBC television interview broadcast on 17 October 1968, Lewis spoke with terrifying eloquence on the recurring themes of this article: drowned valleys, the need for political violence, and of blood sacrifice in the name of the nation:

> Saunders Lewis: 'I personally believe that careful, considered public violence is often a necessary weapon for national movements, necessary to defend the land, the valleys of Wales from being violated, wholly illegally, by the government and the big corporations in England. I think, for instance, that Tryweryn, Clywedog, Cwm Dulas, are attacks that cannot be justified on moral grounds at all. The fact that they were decided on by the English Parliament confers no moral right. And so I think that any means that hinders this irresponsible violence on the land of Wales by English corporations, is wholly just.'
>
> Meirion Edwards: 'Do you include the shedding of blood?'
> Saunders Lewis: 'So long as it is Welsh blood and not English blood.'[45]

('Too long a sacrifice/Can make a stone of the heart.')

Saunders Lewis is the very archetype for the problematic, displaced Welsh nationalist leader, positioning himself at several removes from the mainstream of Welsh identity as it had become constructed across the nineteenth century: he was English-born, Catholic, urban, high-cultural, European, aristocratic; as T. Robin Chapman, his biographer, suggests, this sense of cultural displacement may be the key to understanding Lewis, who described himself 'fel un "sy'n bererin yng Nghymru"' (as one who is a pilgrim in Wales), and who is at once the greatest, and the least typical, of all Welsh Nationalists.

A literary geomancer, I would suggest, could plot a line of force – a ley-line – running contiguous with the Welsh border, moving from Avebury to Caerleon to Crybbe to Wallasey to Alderley Edge. I would propose, in fact, that we redraw this line as constituting the Welsh border proper, or more precisely as the outer limit of a permeable borderline which often moves many miles beyond Offa's Dyke, and which renders identity as nebulous, hybrid, plural. Popular culture is good at fingering anxieties, though not necessarily at providing coherent solutions. Welsh nationalist horror, like Welsh nationalism itself, may finally be unassimilable within the confines of the nation as it is currently configured, but a too-rigorous concentration on borders as final markers of identity limits the imagination, and closes off possibilities.

NOTES

This article was first given as a paper in the symposium 'Wales, Ireland and Popular Culture' at the University of Cardiff, September 24, 2010. I would like to thank Dr Katie Gramich and Dr Claire Connolly for inviting me to this event. My thanks also to Professor Jane Aaron for drawing my attention to the existence of *The Knighton Vampires*, and for suggesting that I might want to look again at the works of Islwyn Ffowc Elis.

1 W. B. Yeats, *Collected Poems*, ed. Augustine Martin (London: Vintage, 1992), p. 350.

2 This argument about the centralising stability of realist fiction is adapted from Raymond Williams, *The Country and the City* (London: Hogarth Press, 1973).

3 See Saunders Lewis, 'The Fate of the Language', trans. G. Aled Williams, in Alun R. Jones and Gwyn Thomas, eds, *Presenting Saunders Lewis* (Cardiff: University of Wales Press, 1983), pp. 127-41; Ned Thomas, *The Welsh Extremist: Modern Welsh Politics, Literature and Society* (Talybont: Y Lolfa, 1991), first published under the title *The Welsh Extremist: A Culture in Crisis* in 1971.

4 For accounts of direct action Welsh nationalist groups, see Roy Clews, *To Dream of Freedom: The Story of MAC and the Free Wales Army* (Talybont: Y Lolfa: 2004); John Humphries, *Freedom Fighters: Wales's Forgotten 'War', 1963-1993* (Cardiff: University of Wales Press, 2008).
5 Humphries, p. 106.
6 Ibid., p. 146.
7 See Thomas, *The Welsh Extremist*, p. 17.
8 Humphries, pp. 67-8.
9 T. Robin Chapman, *Un Bywyd o Blith Nifer: Cofiant Saunders Lewis* [*One Life Amongst Several: A Biography of Saunders Lewis*] (Llandysul: Gomer, 2006), pp. 326, 331.
10 Ibid., p. 329.
11 Ibid., p. 356.
12 Rob Lewis, 'The Pattern Under the Plough', *Sight and Sound*, 20:8 (August 2010), 16-22.
13 For an account of the making of *The Wicker Man*, see Allan Brown, *The Wicker Man: The Morbid Ingenuities* (London: Sidgwick and Jackson, 2000).
14 See Darryl Jones, 'Borderlands: Spiritualism and the Occult in Fin-de-siècle and Edwardian Welsh and Irish Horror', *Irish Universities Review*, 17:1 (2009), pp. 31-44.
15 Sigmund Freud, *The Standard Edition of the Complete Psychological Works of Sigmund Freud vol. XXIII: Moses and Monotheism, An Outline of Psycho-Analysis and Other Works*, ed. and trans. James Strachey et al (London: Vintage, 2001), p. 17.
16 I am not the first person to apply *Moses and Monotheism* to the nationalisms of these islands: see (although to very different ends and in a very different context) W. J. McCormack, 'Robert Emmet and Roger Casement', in Anne Dolan, Patrick Geoghegan and Darryl Jones, eds, *Reinterpreting Emmet: Essays on the Life and Legacy of Robert Emmet* (Dublin: UCD Press, 2007), pp. 219-26.
17 Ernest Renan, *The Poetry of the Celtic Races: and other studies*, translated, with introduction and notes, by William G. Hutchinson (London: Walter Scott, Ltd., 1896). This

essay was an important influence on Yeats, notably for his own essay on 'The Celtic Element in Literature'.

18 Yeats, op. cit., p. 177.

19 Alfred Watkins, *The Old Straight Track: Its Mounds, Beacons, Moats, Sites and Mark Stones* (London: Abacus, 1974 [1925]), p. 83.

20 Ibid., p. 215.

21 T. Robin Chapman, *Rhywfaint o Anfarwoldeb: Bywgraffiad Islawyn Ffowc Elis* [*Some Measure of Immortality: A Biography of Islwyn Ffowc Elis*] (Llandysul: Gomer, 2003), p. 22.

22 Islwyn Ffowc Elis, *Y Gromlech yn yr Haidd* (1970; Llandysul: Gomer, 1988), pp. 21, 64, 12.

23 Ibid., p. 31.

24 Ibid., p. 83.

25 Saunders Lewis, 'The Caernarfon Court Speech', in, *Presenting Saunders Lewis*, p. 126.

26 Julian Richards, interviewed by Anthony Brockway, http://homepage.ntlworld.com/elizabeth.ercocklly/julian.htm. (accessed 19 September, 2010).

27 Phil Rickman, *Candlenight* (London: Pan, 1993), p. 371.

28 Ibid., p. 319. As if it needed underlining, the follow-up comment is 'Never read R. S. Thomas?'

29 Ibid., p. 307.

30 Ibid., pp. 288-9.

31 Phil Rickman, *Crybbe* (London: Pan, 1993), p. 183.

32 Guy N. Smith, *The Knighton Vampires* (London: Piatkus, 1993), pp. 11, 9.

33 Ibid., p. 28.

34 Ibid., p. 113.

35 Ibid., p. 82.

36 Ibid., pp. 97-8.

37 Phil Rickman, *The Man in the Moss* (London: Pan, 1994), pp. 157, 245.

38 Ibid., p. 69.

39 Alan Garner, 'Postrcript' to *The Owl Service* (1967; London: HarperCollins, 2007), p. 222.

40 Ibid., p. 60.
41 Ibid., p. 86.
42 Ibid., pp. 32, 61-2.
43 Ibid., pp. 136, 138-9.
44 Saunders Lewis, 'Blodeuwedd', in *Y Casgliad Cyflawn: Cyfrol 1*, ed. Ioan M Williams (Cardiff: University of Wales Press, 1996) p. 259.
45 This translation in Ned Thomas, *The Welsh Extremist*, p. 69.
46 T. Robin Chapman, *Un Bywyd o Blith Nifer*, p. 10.

"Mixed-Up Creatures":

Identity and its boundaries in Arthur Machen's weird tales

Jessica George
Cardiff University

In this essay, I shall be discussing two short stories by Arthur Machen, who was an early writer of what has come to be known as 'weird fiction', and an acknowledged influence upon better-known exponents of the genre. Machen may have his place in the Welsh canon, but when we see him mentioned in criticism, it is often as a minor decadent or Victorian gothic writer.[1] The weird tale certainly contains its gothic elements, and its preoccupation with the rupturing of the borders of identity is one with clear roots in the gothic tradition. I believe that there is, however, a distinct manner of looking at these ruptures that characterizes the weird tale. H. P. Lovecraft, a fellow weird author and a devotee of Machen's work, perhaps encapsulates this viewpoint best when he writes:

> The true weird tale has something more than secret murder, bloody bones, or a sheeted form clanking chains according to rule. A certain atmosphere of breathless and unexplainable dread of outer, unknown forces must be present; and there must be a hint, expressed with a seriousness and portentousness becoming its subject, of that most terrible conception of the human brain – a malign and particular suspension or defeat of those fixed laws of Nature which are our only safeguard against the assault of chaos and the daemons of unplumbed space.[2]

Lovecraft here uses the term 'malign' – but elsewhere, he describes the impulse behind his writing as the desire to 'achieve, momentarily, the illusion of some strange suspension or violation of the galling limitations of time, space, and natural law which for ever imprison us and frustrate our curiosity', and tells us that these stories are horror stories only because 'fear is our deepest and strongest emotion, and the one which best lends itself to the creation of nature-defying illusions'.[3] These are two quite different characterisations of the same literary effect, but I do not think that either is incorrect. The two interpretations exist variously, and sometimes simultaneously, in much weird fiction. It is this ambivalence, this expression of scientific awe alongside fear, that characterises the weird tale's treatment of identity – particularly human identity – and the places in which it is called into question.

Of course, Decadent literature and horror fiction, two genres in which we might place Machen's work, have never been entirely respectable. There is a whiff of sensation about them, a sense that their fantastic happenings and grotesque beings render them not entirely worthy of serious consideration. And trashiness is not the worst accusation that has been levelled at them. We are accustomed to newspaper articles suggesting that horror films and comic books are a threat to the moral fabric of society, but the idea that disreputable fiction might actually occasion a nation- or continent-wide spiral of moral and intellectual decline has a long history, finding its antecedents in Max Nordau's 1892 study *Degeneration*, in which he suggests that the work of degenerate artists (among whom he numbers figures as diverse as Ibsen, Wagner, Nietzsche, and the French Decadents) is precipitating the downfall of Western Europe, and must be suppressed.[4] In Britain, at least, the association of 'degenerate' aesthetic movements – particularly the Decadent movement, of which Machen is often classed as a member – with behaviour perceived as immoral seemed to be cemented by the trials of Oscar Wilde and, in the wake of the trials, Machen himself had difficulty publishing his work for almost a decade.[5] The stories examined here make heavy use of folkloric stories about the fairies, or Little People, and the association of fairy beliefs with supposedly undesirable, 'degenerate', or undeveloped groups of people is perhaps not irrelevant here. Fairy beliefs were predominantly present in working-class, Celtic areas of the British Isles, newspaper reports of changelings being most frequent in these areas, and poor Celtic and Roman Catholic people were viewed as inherently credulous, weak in character and morality.[6] At the same time, however, the reports of changelings – who were described in terms familiar from xenophobic racial stereotypes, with their dark hair and eyes, sallow skins, and sly behaviour – seemed to prove the inferiority of these groups.[7] These creatures were most common in Ireland, and the frequency with which they appeared seemed, for some folklorists, to lend credence to the notion that Irish people were primitive and inferior.[8] Fairy beliefs, then, were considered the province of the evolutionarily backward. But, at the same time, they fed off and fed into wider cultural narratives about race, humanity, and evolution. I would like to suggest that Machen's weird tales, also condemned as the products and preferred entertainment of inferior minds, did much the same thing.

In 'The Novel of the Black Seal', as Kirsti Bohata has rightly noted, racial and degenerative fears are mapped onto the figure of the fairy in straightforwardly horrific fashion, drawing upon 'racist colonial discourses' for its effect. The tale, Bohata suggests, may be 'problematic for Welsh readers who find themselves excluded from the implied audience', and can be read as 'expressive of the fears of a "border" identity, who wants to be "English" (the superior race) but fears he is contaminated by (undesirable) Welshness.'[9] Certainly, 'The Novel of the Black Seal' seems, for the most part, to identify with those English colonial and racial discourses from whose implied audience Machen, a native of (the 'wrong' side of) the England-Wales border, might have found himself excluded. Not all of his fiction, however, is so straightforward in its treatment of racial and non-'human' Others. (The 'human', it should be noted, both in Machen's fiction and in the Western late-Victorian scientific discourses upon which he draws, is more accurately described as the white, Western, educated, and usually male 'human'.) I would like to suggest that 'The White People,' a later tale which makes use of similar elements from British fairylore, displays a profound, if not explicit, ambivalence towards identities which threaten the 'human'. Like 'The Novel of the Black Seal', it ties in with contemporary historical, scientific and pseudo-scientific narratives of threat to 'human' identity, and to anthropocentric conceptions of the universe in a post-Darwin age. It is similarly concerned with exposing the boundaries of what is 'human' as unstable, and perhaps ultimately untenable. It is framed by a discussion about the nature of evil, and certainly contains its fair share of grotesque imagery. But it appears far less certain of the non-human as a threat – or, perhaps more accurately, far less certain that what is under threat should be preserved. At the borderlands of identity, it would seem, attitudes are similarly unstable and unfixed.

In order to understand the ways in which Machen makes use of the figure of the fairy, it is necessary first to understand the ways in which contemporary accounts of the origins of fairy beliefs positioned the fairy as a threat to ideas about the nature and status of humanity. The 'Turanian dwarf theory', developed by euhemerist folklorists of the nineteenth century, drew on evolutionary theory, placing the fairy and the human in continuity with each other, and raising the horrific regressive possibilities of the evolutionary narrative. This theory posited that traditional fairy beliefs constituted a folk memory of conquered aboriginal peoples who had fled into remote areas to escape the invading Celts. This theory seemed to find confirmation in Western encounters with African 'pygmy' tribes during the 1880s. Victorian anthropologists viewed these people as missing links, 'among the earliest, hence crudest of the human species',[10] and even debated whether they were fully human. Contemporary accounts of the 'pygmies' ascribed to them many of the traits commonly associated with supernatural dwarves and fairies. Carole G. Silver, in her wide-ranging study *Strange and Secret Peoples*, attributes this view to a sort of 'cultural slippage', and it is true that anthropological accounts from the period do seem to conflate pygmies and fairies, sometimes even going so far as to make the comparison explicitly. Sir Harry Johnston, for example, says that the pygmies remind him 'over and over again of the traits attributed to the brownies and goblins of our fairy stories' while Sidney Hinde calls them 'gnome-like beings'.[11]

At the same time, traits associated with 'lower' or 'less evolved' humans became associated with and ascribed to the fairies of folklore. *Fin-de-siècle* dwarfs and fairies lost their individuality, and became a 'horde', devoid of humanising traits, 'hunting in packs and skulking in shadows, threatening to destroy or subvert the ruling race'. Fairies had traditionally been considered as lacking souls and as incapable of feeling true emotion; now, even distinct personalities and faces were denied them. They came to be described in terms more commonly associated with animals, Darwinian human ancestors and 'primitive' groups. The existence of the 'pygmies' seemed to confirm both evolutionary theory and the reality of the fairies – or, at least, that of their pre-human originals. And when the fairies became real, they became frightening. Fiction of the late Victorian period and the early part of the twentieth century portrayed the fairies in new and horrific ways. Machen's short stories contain several examples of portrayals of a malign or ambiguous surviving prehistoric race, as well as suggesting the persistence of pre-Christian spirituality or ritual in the areas where the fairies survive.

'The Novel of the Black Seal' gives us a portrayal of the

fairies in which we can clearly identify the biological fears stemming from evolutionary theory and embodied in the figure of the fairy as prehistoric survival. Machen's Little People are here malign, grotesque, bestial, even predatory, seizing on unwary humans to use for their own purposes. But the simple physical threat they pose to those unlucky enough to encounter them was not the primary source of horror for their audience; rather, it was the evidence of human descent from lower primates and the suggestion of chaotic evolutionary potential constituted by their very existence that was truly to terrify Machen's readers.

The non-linear nature of evolutionary development meant that degeneration and atavism were seen as very real possibilities, and Kelly Hurley discusses the endemic cultural anxieties engendered by such felt threats in her book, *The Gothic Body*. If the human was the product of a random and unfinished process, then humanity's continuing supremacy and progress was by no means assured, and a number of horrific potential outcomes suggested themselves: perhaps the human species was not yet fully evolved in itself, not yet fully 'human'; perhaps other animal species might continue to evolve and eventually overtake us, destabilising human centrality on Earth; or perhaps evolution itself was reversible. In the end, we might 'retrogress into a sordid animalism rather than progress towards a telos of intellectual and moral perfection'.[13] The figure of the fairy is a physical reminder of this process, and of our origins, and as such has the ability to destabilise the identity of the human subject. Indeed, when Machen's characters encounter the fairies, their own humanness and civilised nature is frequently called into question, blurred around the edges. Contact with these Little People has a degenerative effect.

Like most of Machen's Little People stories, 'The Novel of the Black Seal' takes place in an area where civilisation is beginning to disappear into the wilderness, where the human world is represented only by small settlements or lone houses, and where the wild countryside surrounding it looms large and threatening. It is set in the Gwent area around Machen's hometown of Caerleon – close to the border with England – and this area is familiar ground to any reader acquainted with Machen's work. For the purposes of the story, however, Machen adds an aura of the sinister, suggesting that the enchantment the landscape holds is not necessarily a benign one. Miss Lally, the story's narrator, finds herself oppressed by it, saying 'here in this lonely house, shut in on all sides by the olden woods and the vaulted hills, terror seems to spring inconsequent from every covert, and the flesh is aghast at the half-heard murmurs of horrible things'.[14] She feels 'imprisoned amidst the ancient woods, shut in an olden land of mystery and dread, and as if all was long ago and forgotten by the living outside'.[15] It is suggested to us, then, that here the present is very much continuous with the ancient past; that there is very little in the way of separation between the sparse human settlements and a much older, more hostile world. Certainly this is a liminal location, a borderland, like many of the places in which fairies traditionally appear, but here, borders themselves (between past and present, civilisation and wilderness) seem unsettlingly permeable. This wild landscape with its generalized, not-quite-definable menace takes on a life of its own, and highlights how ephemeral and relatively recent the human presence here is, and how easily it might be ousted. The fitness of humans to inhabit this landscape is implicitly questioned. Will we survive? Are we the fittest?

Long-held assumptions about the status and nature of humanity are dissolved here, just as they are in scientific narratives about evolution and degeneration. The human no longer holds its default position at the centre of the universe, and the rest of that universe is no longer relevant only in terms of its relationship to humanity. Rather, humans have to begin to view themselves in terms of their relationship to a world no longer designed specifically for them, in which they hold a position no more secure than that of the so-called lower species. In Hurley's words, 'as "the human" loses its particularity, it also begins to be evacuated of its meaningfulness. A Darwinian Nature does not privilege, indeed takes no particular notice of, the human species'. And if nature accords us no specific privilege, we can no longer be sure that the position the human species holds – or even the form it takes – will remain constant.

The references to traditional fairylore that occur in 'The Novel of the Black Seal' are not limited to descriptions of the landscape. The strangeness of Jervase Cradock, the half-fairy child implicitly conceived by rape when his mother was attacked while walking in a remote area, recalls numerous folk descriptions of changelings thought to have replaced normal, healthy, human babies. The changeling is often discovered through its unnatural speech, and during his fits, Cradock emits utterances in the inhuman, hissing language of the Little People, a 'jargon but little removed from the inarticulate noises of brute beasts'.[17] We are encouraged to be repulsed by Cradock and, by extension, by his non-human parentage, precisely in the way that he possesses enough human attributes to make his inhuman aspects jarringly incongruous – uncanny, perhaps – a distorted echo or mirror-image.

Even Cradock, however, is half human. The story avoids showing us the Little People directly, and the ultimate fate of Professor Gregg, who we are led to believe has been abducted and horribly transformed by them, is only implied. The tactic of avoiding description, of telling us that the story's ultimate horror is simply unspeakable, is a common feature of the weird tale and may actually work in the story's favour here, as it tells us that the Little People defy classification, that they exist on a borderland for which there are no words.

It is traditional that those who have visited fairyland are never quite the same when they return home, having been cursed or irrevocably altered by the experience, and that the fairies possess preternatural powers which they use to effect this transformation. These fairies, however, are not just a race of mischievous imps; they wreak real, physical harm on those unfortunate enough to encounter them. The curse which remains with those who survive is permanent, and cannot be lifted by magic. It is their world-view, their self-concept, which has been irreversibly changed. The curse is the knowledge of human origin, and the possibility that the ancestor, the degenerative germ, has existed within us all along.

The slimy tentacle produced by Cradock's body when Professor Gregg reads a particular inscription illustrates the mutability of the body, recalling the formless, uncontained matter or 'primordial slime' of life's origin, holding all forms in potential, occupying the border between liquid and solid, never quite one or the other but always threatening to change. It is matter in the process of solidifying or of dissolving, suggesting the ephemerality of form, the possibility that we ourselves may quite easily be broken down and reformed into a quite different shape. The story's suggestion that the Little People have incantations that can cause the human body to revert to 'the slime from which [it] came'[18] reminds us of this fact, and suggests to us that the body itself – which, after all, contains a fair amount of slimy matter – has no real integrity, and may break down or be swallowed up into amorphousness.

The physical form of the Little People, and the repulsiveness of their practices, elicit strong reactions from Machen's late-Victorian observers. After the aforementioned incident with Cradock, the unfortunate maid who lands the task of cleaning up is repulsed by a 'queer ... bad smell' and reports that it made her feel 'very sick'.[19] Nausea is an intensely physical experience, and here it effectively forces the human subject back into the body, acting as a reminder of materiality, of our inability to separate ourselves from a body that is instinctive, animal, in its responses. It is not only working-class characters – viewed as closer to the primitive, more likely to be superstitious and to believe in fairies in the first place – who are at risk, however.

We know that the Little People possess incantations which can reduce the human subject to pre-human form, forcing him to 'put on the flesh of the reptile and the snake',[20] and we are led to believe that this is what has happened to Professor Gregg after his disappearance. We should note that when Cradock transforms, his descent towards the reptilian is not straightforwardly imposed from the outside. The slimy tentacle that he extends comes *out* of the body, implying a calling-forth of something already extant, in latent form, within him. It is perhaps not too far-fetched to say that there is a similar implication in the way that Gregg's seeking after scientific proof, after knowledge – the very hallmark of the 'civilized' subject – leads to his physical descent on the evolutionary scale. Some innate component of the human body or mind seems to be perpetually harking back to the biological past, always mutable, never settled or fully 'human'. The potential for reversion is contained within every human subject, the privileges of class and education providing scant protection. Here is the ultimate horror of 'The Novel of the Black Seal' and its notion of the pre-human survival. What we should fear is not the swallowing-up of the human subject by something else, or the possibility that the Little People may transform us into something other than what we are. Rather, the most awful of possible outcomes is that they will reveal what has been there all along – that we are already them.

This notion of dangerous knowledge, then, is an important factor in the dissolution of human identity, in the atavistic reversion of the human subject. The idea of a forbidden tradition, a handing-down of hidden information, is also one that Machen uses frequently, the transformative spell in 'The Novel of the Black Seal' being one of several examples.

The idea of a pre-Christian pagan religion in Western Europe was a commonly accepted one during the twentieth century, and was thought to be the basis of many stories about witches and devil-worshippers.[21] The Church, the theory runs, incorporated the horned god of the old religion into its own mythology as the Devil, and demonized and persecuted its practitioners accordingly. This theory is elaborated in the works of the anthropologist Margaret Murray, who may, in fact, have been familiar with and influenced by Machen's fiction. The rites and practices we see in Machen's Little People stories are clearly placed as pre-Christian, and are linked to the transformative – or revelatory – power the Little People seem to hold over human identity. D. P. M. Michael, writing in 1971, points out that Machen sometimes 'attempts to get his horrific effects by encouraging the notion that ... their practices are still carried on among us',[22] or, in other words, that modern, civilized 'human' identity has something older and darker, something predating the 'human', beneath its surface. Machen wrote some shorter prose pieces on this theme, but develops it most fully in 'The White People', composed in the late 1890s. The tale is certainly sinister, and the principal narrator's fear of a sexually threatening 'Black Man' suggests that it is indebted to some of the same racialised discourses. The struggle with identity occurring here is, however, focused slightly differently from that in 'The Novel of the Black Seal', and seems far more ambiguous, relying on a kind of mystic awe rather than physical horror for its uncanny effects.

The main body of 'The White People' is the 'Green Book narrative', a diary kept by a young girl who has since committed suicide, detailing her experiences with various arcane rituals, fairylike beings, and enchanted areas of the countryside. In some ways, it appears to take the form of a coming-of-age or sexual-awakening narrative, the narrator's sensual fascination with the strange new country she discovers and her fear of the 'Black Man' who may come to claim her for his wife representing conflicting feelings about her journey towards adulthood. It certainly seems significant that her experiences take place during adolescence, at a time when identity is still in the process of being formed. Children and young people were traditionally seen as those most at risk of fairy abduction, not yet being fully integrated into the adult world, and Haeckel's theory of recapitulation, not then refuted, might suggest a similar view of the young in the scientific community.[23] If the organism passes through more primitive stages of development during its growth, then the child is an imperfectly evolved creature, perhaps not yet fully human. If we take this view, the narrator is not merely on the verge of adulthood: she is on the verge of becoming human.

Unlike the unfortunate victims of the Little People – Jervase Cradock's mother, for example – the narrator of 'The White People' is seemingly complicit in her own involvement with the old religion, actively seeking out the fairies' forbidden knowledge rather than being attacked or abducted, or stumbling across them unwittingly. We see relatively little of the narrator's life outside her experiences with the old religion, but what we do find out makes it appear restricted, even stultifying. The Green Book narrative begins with the narrator's assertion that she found the notebook when '[i]t was a very rainy day and [she] could not go out',[24] and she goes on to tell us that she is unable to share the secrets that she knows, and that other people don't understand the rituals she performs. The sparse detailing of her day-to-day existence makes it far less vivid and engaging than the occasions on which she meets the fairies, practises their rituals, and journeys into their lands. Perhaps, then, it is unsurprising that, rather than taking her assigned place in the properly socialised adult world, she chooses pagan ritual and uncontained sexuality, characteristics usually associated with 'primitive' tribes and peoples of the distant past. Her inability to share her experiences keeps a channel of communication between her and the human world closed, and it is significant that her experiences are figured as a physical journey; she literally moves away from the human world, turning towards the 'primitive' rather than becoming civilized.

Her knowledge, however, is not entirely learned. It rather seems to have been something innate in her, something she has been familiar with since early childhood, forgetting bits and pieces of it as she grows older, and reconnecting with it in the amorphous, uncertain years before adulthood.[25] Early childhood is portrayed as a kind of uncivilised, undefined state, during which she is at one with the White People of the title. They watch her in her cradle and tell her stories; she learns the 'Xu language' in which they speak; and as a still young child she sees them 'play and dance and sing' in a wood near her home. Her childhood interactions with them are described simply, without comment, and flow naturally in the narrative – which itself seems to recall an undifferentiated state of being in its very long sentences and endless accumulations of description. If anything, the narrator recalls the White People with fondness. This seemingly harmless nostalgia for infancy contrasts vividly, however, with the way in which the narrative is framed, as will become clear.

The Green Book is brought up as a piece of evidence in a discussion between two men, Ambrose and Cotgrave, about the nature of evil. Ambrose elaborates his theory of evil, asserting that it can best be defined as 'the taking of Heaven by storm', the attempt to penetrate into a sphere higher than that ordained to humans. The passage in which he attempts to explain this to Cotgrave is frequently quoted to illustrate what is meant by the 'weird' in 'weird fiction', and is worth repeating here:

> What would your feelings be, seriously, if your cat or your

> dog began to talk to you, and to dispute with you in human accents? You would be overwhelmed with horror. I am sure of it. And if the roses in your garden sang a weird song, you would go mad. And suppose the stones in the road began to swell and grow before your eyes, and if the pebble that you noticed at night had shot out stony blossoms in the morning?[27]

Evil, in other words, is what we see when objects or life-forms behave in ways we would expect of other, more complex and highly-developed beings or organisms. Sanctity, or ultimate good, in contrast, consists in an endeavour to recapture Edenic bliss; in a return to origin.

However, the narrator of the Green Book appears to have held the knowledge she seeks, at least in part, since early childhood, and there are hints, in the passing-down of secrets by the nurse and her foremothers, that these are the last fragments of an ancient religion, something perhaps once known to all humankind. If this is correct, then she is in fact seeking to return to Eden – the unbounded, undifferentiated bliss of infancy – rather than to discover a new and forbidden sphere. The Green Book narrative itself seems to undercut and to query Ambrose's definitions, for if the old religion is something ingrained in the human race, then Ambrose's delineation of the correct, natural human sphere is a false, arbitrary one. We might begin to question the naturalness of the distinction itself.

At the end of the Green Book narrative, the girl appears to be communicating more and more often with the 'nymphs' or supernatural beings, and withdraws almost completely into the world of her secrets. The final revelation, however, is only hinted at. The girl recalls the white lady she saw as a small child in the wood, and tells us that she 'knew who the white lady was' after looking into a well. The implication here seems to be that what she sees is her own reflection, that the 'White People' of the title are not mysterious, wholly Other beings, but ourselves.

The story's epilogue returns to the dangerous knowledge theme, with Ambrose suggesting that some of the mysteries hinted at in the Green Book will eventually be illuminated by science. There are, he tells us:

> references throughout the manuscript to certain "processes" which have been handed down by tradition from age to age. Some of these processes are just beginning to come within the purview of science, which has arrived at them – or rather at the steps which lead to them – by quite different paths. I have interpreted the reference to "nymphs" as a reference to one of these processes.[28]

Once again, progress and investigation are raised as potential catalysts of humanity's dissolution. Ambrose argues, in essence, that only the correct individuals – educated, 'civilised' ones, presumably – are qualified to seek the truth. Knowledge is as dangerous as an unlocked medicine cabinet to those without the proper qualifications; experimenting at random, 'the child may find the key by chance, and drink herself dead'. The 'child' here, we infer, does not refer simply to the girl in the Green Book, but to humanity as a whole.[29] In those too imperfectly civilised, the search may result in an awful descent into 'evil'.

We learn, finally, that the girl who wrote the Green Book committed suicide a year later, and was found dead before a pagan image in the woods. Ambrose states that she 'poisoned herself – in time', implying that a fate worse than death was about to befall her. Was she to be taken by the black man, or discovered as a witch and punished accordingly? Lost in fairyland and permanently isolated from humanity? Would she have become something other than human? The ending appears, at first glance, to reinforce Ambrose's morality, but the ending of the Green Book narrative itself suggests that perhaps the old religion and the secrets of the white people are as natural, as essentially human, as anything – including the behaviours of 'civilised' man. From one point of view, it is they that constitute the search for Eden. How natural is human nature as we define it? The two narratives exist in tension with one another, and while we must agree with Ambrose that the girl's death is not the ultimate horror of the story, it is not her impertinence in pursuing a hidden knowledge that gives the story its sense of unease, but its implicit questioning of what, exactly, is human and natural.

The story's suggestion that the 'white lady' exists in us already is not so different from the suggestion in 'The Novel of the Black Seal' that we may all have the potential for terrifying evolutionary reversions. But its presentation is, I think, more complex. 'The Novel of the Black Seal' seems to suggest a need for constant vigilance against atavism, and a stark warning against the pursuit of dangerous knowledge, lest we suffer the fate of Professor Gregg. 'The White People', however, in implicitly questioning its own definitions of 'evil', seems to suggest that, perhaps, those aspects of our nature dismissed as atavistic or uncivilised are as natural as any others. Certainly, as Bohata suggests regarding 'The Novel of the Black Seal', it might be possible to read 'The White People' as the product of a border identity at odds with itself. I would not wish to suggest that it be read as a post-colonial text, or one particularly celebratory of Welshness, but it evidences a struggle with, rather than a dismissal of, the repressed, 'undesirable' identity. While it is framed by a discourse of 'evil' that supports the colonial, anthropocentric narrative, it is never far from acknowledging an attraction to the racialised, de-'human'-ised Other within.

NOTES

1 Machen garners brief mentions in Nicholas Ruddick's essay, 'The fantastic fiction of the fin de siècle' in Gail Marshall, ed., *The Cambridge Companion to the Fin de Siècle* (Cambridge: Cambridge University Press, 2007) and in Fred Botting's *Gothic* (London: Routledge, 1996). A slightly longer discussion appears in Linda Dryden's *The Modern Gothic and Literary Doubles* (Basingstoke: Palgrave MacMillan, 2003), where she characterises him as a gothic writer heavily influenced by Stevenson.

2 *Supernatural Horror in Literature*, (New York: Dover, 1973), p. 15.

3 'Notes on Writing Weird Fiction', in *Collected Essays, Vol. 2: Literary Criticism*, ed. S. T. Joshi (New York: Hippocampus Press, 2004), p. 176.

4 Max Nordau, *Degeneration*, (London: University of Nebraska Press, 1993), pp. 556-560.

5 http://www.machensoc.demon.co.uk/machbiog.html (Accessed 07 September, 2010).

6 Carole G. Silver, *Strange and Secret Peoples: Fairies and Victorian Consciousness* (Oxford: Oxford University Press, 1999), p. 67.

7 Silver, p. 86.

8 Silver, p. 67.

9 Kirsti Bohata, 'Apes and Cannibals in Cambria: Images of the Racial and Gendered Other in Gothic Writing in Wales', *Welsh Writing in English*, 6 (2000), 119-143 (p. 126).

10 Silver, p. 130.

11 Ibid., pp. 130-136.

12 Ibid., pp. 146-147.

13 Kelly Hurley, *The Gothic Body: Sexuality, Materialism and Degeneration at the* Fin de Siècle (Cambridge: Cambridge University Press, 1996), p. 56.

14 Arthur Machen, *The Three Impostors* (London: John Baker, 1964), p. 104.

15 Ibid., p. 105.

16 Hurley, p. 61.

17 Machen, *The Three Impostors*, p. 111.
18 Ibid., p. 120.
19 Ibid., p. 103.
20 Ibid., p. 120.
21 D. P. M. Michael, *Arthur Machen*, (Cardiff: University of Wales Press, 1971), pp. 16-17.
22 Ibid., p. 17.
23 Ernst Haeckel, *The Evolution of Man: A Popular Scientific Study*, trans. by Joseph McCabe (London: Watts & Co., 1912), I, p. 1.
24 Arthur Machen, 'The White People', in *The Great God Pan*, (Cardigan: Parthian, 2010), p. 124.
25 Ibid., p. 125.
26 Ibid., p. 126.
27 Ibid., pp. 116-117.
28 Ibid., p. 163.
29 Ibid., p. 164.

Minstrelsy in Malcolm Pryce's *Aberystwyth Mon Amour*

Catherine Phelps
Cardiff University

In a discussion about Welsh crime fiction and its use of place, Stephen Knight asks if the use of a 'zero-setting' by the writer Bill James 'may be...a wish to avoid the stage-Welsh effect of much south Welsh writing (including Dylan Thomas's prose) which is felt to be a cringingly colonial performance.'[1] Knight also proposes that zero-settings for Welsh crime writers could increase their marketability, a suggestion reinforced by crime novelists who have told how publishing houses discouraged them from setting their work in Wales,[2] for as the author David Williams was told, '[n]obody commits crimes in Wales!'[3] Welsh devolution appears to mark a turning point, though, since shortly after the 'yes' vote, Wales becomes a primary crime scene for many native writers. Jane Aaron has drawn parallels between devolution and a growth in Welsh cultural confidence, suggesting that it encouraged writers to set their work in their native country. She has said of the opening night of the Welsh Assembly in 1999, '[i]mages associated with that evening's concert – of the red dragon in flames over Cardiff Bay, for example, or draped over Shirley Bassey as she sang in her birthplace – appeared to many as symbols of a regenerated Wales, embarked on a new mode of existence promising greater national self-determination in spheres not restricted to the political.'[4] Aaron's 'greater national self-determination' may partly account for this new visibility of Wales in crime fiction but English publishing houses, such as Bloomsbury and Serpent's Tail,[5] must have also recognised the increasing marketability of a devolved nation as both now publish crime fiction set in Wales.

Moreover, Wales does not simply act as a picturesque stage set in these works, for place becomes central in the crime novel. Of course, this phenomenon is not restricted solely to Wales. Commentators, such as Eva Erdman, have argued that place and the cultural specificity associated with setting, has become the focal point of much late twentieth-century crime fiction, rather than the act of crime. Citing Henning Mankell's *Wallander* series and the work of German writer Jakob Arjouni as examples, Erdman explains that:

> [t]he reading of crime novels becomes an ethnographic reading; the scene of the crime becomes the locus genius of the cultural tragedy...gradually at first, and then increasingly, as the boom in crime fiction took off, the pursuit of the criminal was displaced by the search for cultural identity.[6]

Similarly, post-devolution Welsh crime fiction becomes involved in the examination of cultural identity and foregrounds its own cultural specificity.

Consequently, crimes are no longer investigated as in the earlier twentieth-century crime fiction that was set in Wales by a visiting English detective but by a native one. Welsh detectives had appeared in print before but, like their English counterparts, were usually at the scene of the crime as visitors only to return to England once order had been restored. Often they were figures of British authority; pre-devolution Welsh detectives were Oxbridge dons,[7] Scotland Yard[8] detectives and merchant bankers.[9] This has been supplanted in many cases by the native Police Procedural; the aforementioned Bill James and David Williams have both created new detective characters sited in South Wales in their later work. It is during this recent period also that the Welsh Private Investigator (P. I.) appears.

The P.I.'s origins in hardboiled fiction are well-documented, not least in Raymond Chandler's own essay,

'The Simple Art of Murder' (1950), in which he cast a critical eye upon contemporaneous detective novels and called for more realism in crime fiction. Chandler provides Dashiell Hammett as an example of how this can be achieved, arguing that his prose was 'spare, frugal, hardboiled.'[10] Already in use for some decades before, the adjective 'hardboiled'[11] soon came to be associated with the type of detective fiction described by Chandler. Such American fiction has had a strong and enduring influence on Welsh writing in English generally. Dylan Thomas's short story, 'Old Garbo' (1939),[12] for example, describes a night spent in the seedy underbelly of Swansea pubs; his narrator apes the stance of an American tough guy and uses the sparse prose of hardboiled fiction for comic effect. Later, Gwyn Thomas employed hardboiled prose to a differing end in his novella, Oscar (1946).[13] Victor Golightly suggests that 'some sense of affinity with American life had gripped [Gwyn Thomas's] imagination' but the American fiction 'that attracted him stayed close to the speech of common people.'[14] This borrowed style gave a sense of verisimilitude to the grim realities of life in the industrialised South Wales valleys during the Depression and implies that the working classes have strong similarities which reach across geographical and cultural divides. More recently, the playwright Ed Thomas engages with American culture and emulates its modes in much of his work. Typically, his *House of America* (1988)[15] uses American culture to discuss and discard old stereotypes of Welsh culture. The resultant hybrid culture is one which moves from its old stasis and provides a new culture with which a younger generation can identify. As Thomas has said:

> [t]he Wales of stereotype, leeks, daffodils, look-you-now-boyo rugby supporters singing Max Boyce songs in three-part harmony while phoning mam to tell her they'll be home for tea and Welsh cakes has gone...So, old Wales is dead and

> new Wales is already a possibility, an eclectic, self-defined Wales with attitude.'[16]

Still, while American culture exerted a strong pull on Welsh writing in English in its search for new identities, it is not until the mid 1980s that the hardboiled detective begins to figure prominently in Welsh crime fiction.[17]

The P.I. does make a brief appearance in pre-devolution Welsh crime fiction. Bernard Knight, better known for his Crowner John medieval mysteries, previously wrote crime novels under the pseudonym of Bernard Picton. One of these early crime novels, *Tiger at Bay* (1970), featured Iago Price, a private investigator. Despite Chandler's dictum that the P.I. should be 'a complete man and a common man and yet an unusual man',[18] Iago is a pale, undernourished imitation of his American predecessors. He is a 'thin, weedy young man with a slight stoop. His head was too big for his neck and was topped by thin hair that matched his feeble moustache.'[19] It is clear that at this stage, although situated near the mean streets of Cardiff's Tiger Bay, the Welsh P.I. is not yet a 'complete man'.

Unlike its American precursor, Welsh hardboiled fiction appears too late to be explained as a reaction to 'Golden Age' crime fiction, a genre which, with its customary country house setting and specifically English middle-class concerns, was perhaps uncongenial to Welsh authors anyway. And while there may be parallels to be drawn between Depression-era America and Margaret Thatcher's Britain, Welsh authors continue to employ the mode of hardboiled fiction in a period that moves beyond the industrial and economic decline of the 1980s to a redeveloped, devolved and more prosperous Wales. I wish to propose that, rather than perceiving the use of hardboiled fiction as indicative of the homogenising power of American culture, its appropriation by Welsh writers might be considered as a useful method of resisting English paradigms. Imitation of a globally dominant culture does not need to be regarded as representing the submersion of Welsh culture, but rather can be seen as what Bill Ashcroft et al describe as a post-colonial act of 'appropriation', a 'seizing [of] the language of the centre and re-placing it in a discourse fully adapted to the colonial place.'[20]

Although his novels are widely read as parodic postmodernist texts, it could be argued that the contemporary writer, Malcolm Pryce, appropriates American hardboiled fiction in order to create a new, culturally specific space for Welsh crime fiction. Like Ed Thomas, Pryce questions traditional tropes of Welsh identity through the appropriation of another culture, suggesting that the traditional tropes root the country in an obsolete past and fail to address contemporary Wales.

'Give me a mint choc chip with a wafer of the Absurd'[21]

Born near the Welsh border in Shrewsbury, Pryce moved to Aberystwyth at an early age. The town became the setting for his series of darkly comic crime novels, most of which were written whilst Pryce was living abroad. *Aberystwyth Mon Amour* (2001) has P.I. Louie Knight investigate a plot by Lovespoon, the Grand Wizard of the Druids and 'messianic Welsh teacher' (21), to return the town to the mythical Cantref-y-Gwaelod[22] by breaching the defences of Nant-y-Moch reservoir and flooding the town. In a similar vein to Dylan Thomas's story, 'Old Garbo', the novels derive their comedy through the marriage of the seemingly opposing tropes of American hardboiled fiction with an exaggerated caricature of Welsh culture. The opening paragraph is indicative of the style throughout the series; the speaker is Louie Knight:

> The thing I remember most about it was walking the entire length of the Prom that morning and not seeing a Druid. Normally when I made my stroll shortly before 9 a.m. I

> would see a few hanging around at Sospan's ice-cream stall, preening themselves in their sharp Swansea suits and teardrop aviator shades. Or they would be standing outside Dai the Custard Pie's joke shop, waiting for him to open so they could buy some more of that soap that makes a person's face go black. (3)

The conceit of a town run by Druids who have formed a mafia-style gang, sets a tone of absurdity which continues throughout the narrative. The Aberystwyth series, whilst retaining the motifs of hardboiled fiction – the Private Eye and the femme fatale, for instance – moves from Chandler's 'mean streets' to the actual geography of the seaside town of Aberystwyth, albeit a fantastical Aberystwyth that is dark and menacing, and peopled with comic grotesques.

Aberystwyth Mon Amour may initially appear to be crime fiction's return to Stephen Knight's 'cringingly colonial performance'; the farcical juxtaposition of the hardboiled novel against a cartoonish Welsh culture provides the comedy in the series. Ludic in its representation of Welsh images, the text is similarly playful in its appropriation of hardboiled tropes. The insertion of 'Aberystwyth' into canonical titles such as *Hiroshima Mon Amour*[23] alerts the reader to the parodic nature of the series, as do the publisher's covers which feature noir-style representations of Louie Knight against an Aberystwyth backdrop.

Pryce's crime parodies have had both precedents and imitators in Wales. James Anderson, who settled in Wales, wrote a series of Golden Age pastiches, the first of which was *The Affair of the Blood-stained Egg Cosy* (1975).[24] As Anderson's tongue-in-cheek title suggests, these parodies point out the petty limitations of some crime fiction genres. Recently, there has been a rash of postmodern parodies featuring Wales as an independent state; Jasper Fforde's *Thursday Next* series, which commenced with *The Eyre Affair* (2001),[25] and Gaynor Madoc Leonard's *The*

Carmarthen Underground (2009)[26] share similarities with Pryce's fiction as they all imagine an anachronistic Welsh state while employing Welsh cultural tropes for comic effect. With the exception of Anderson's work, all these texts were published post-devolution, and each uses the marriage of Wales and crime fiction to differing ends.

While there can be little doubt that the novels in Pryce's Aberystwyth series are primarily comic works, it can be argued that Pryce's appropriation of the hardboiled style, meshed with traditional Welsh tropes and a 'wafer of the Absurd' may have a more serious intent in unsettling traditional, stereotyped images of Wales, particularly those prevalent in English metropolitan culture. Clare Morgan, in *The Times Literary Supplement*, described the novel as mixing 'satire, farce, fantasy and comic strip in a world where the Famous Five meet Raymond Chandler.'[27] Although Morgan's reference to Enid Blyton here may not be intentionally derogatory, Welsh culture has routinely been marginalised and belittled by discourses that draw on such infantilising images. *The Sunday Times* columnist A. A. Gill has acquired notoriety through his vituperative attacks on Wales, for example. Famously he once referred to Meibion Glyndŵr, or in Gill's preferred translation, the Sons of Glendower, as 'the Postmen Pat of the international brotherhood of terrorists',[28] an image that deliberately reduces the Welsh to cartoon figures. However, I wish to argue that Pryce, rather than internalising such demeaning tropes and reproducing them in his fiction, is engaged in a complex and subversive act of 'minstrelsy' which challenges such colonial discourses.

The Oxford Companion to Black British History defines 'minstrelsy' as a '[m]usical and humorous entertainment style...The entertainers blacked up, a grotesque parody of black Americans in the Southern slave states.'[29] Early minstrel or blackface performance took elements of black culture, such as speech, songs, and dance, and amplified them, usually to ridicule or infantilise black culture. In this manner, anxieties about the 'Other' are contained and made safe; it is clear that A. A. Gill's fears surrounding Welsh nationalism can easily be incorporated into such a theoretical framework. Like the early minstrel shows of the American South of the mid-nineteenth century which lampooned black Americans through caricature, then, Malcolm Pryce's Aberystwyth novels may also appear to portray a 'grotesque parody' of Welsh culture. However, Pryce's minstrelsy is potentially subversive. Homi K. Bhabha reminds us that 'the *menace* of mimicry is its *double* vision which in disclosing the ambivalence of colonial discourse also disrupts its authority.'[30] Rather than merely internalising and repeating caricatures of Welsh culture, Pryce appropriates and exaggerates these cartoon images and projects them back at those who propagate colonial discourses; the increase in scale also restores the diminished subject and imbues it with an unsettling power.[31]

This magnified cartoon image is exemplified by Pryce's representation of the old women of Aberystwyth, who play a central role in the series. Like Agatha Christie's village spinsters, they are the repository of local history and rumour. Initially depicted as foolish old gossips, the Aberystwyth spinsters and widows nevertheless have a large degree of agency; they are witches, tea-cosy experts, members of an elite commando force drawn from the ranks of the 'Sweet Jesus League' (129). Louie's cleaning woman, Mrs Llantrisant, is central to the plot. Tellingly, not only are her words of direct speech the first the reader hears but they are also in Welsh as she greets Louie with a '*Bore da*'. Despite the occasional Welsh greeting, though, there is little mention of the language in an area where in reality it is very widely spoken. Its fleeting use in the novel suggests that it provides local colour rather than any kind of postcolonial linguistic challenge. Nevertheless, it could be argued that the references in the novel to the runic alphabet, which predates the Roman alphabet still in use today, parallel the fate of the Welsh language. Although runes are part of the school curriculum in *Aberystwyth Mon Amour*, only a small number now understand them. Used by Dai Brainbocs to disguise his proposal for returning Aberystwyth to Cantref-y-Gwaelod, it is also likely that the use of runes is a device to remind readers of Wales's prehistoric and pagan past. However, one of the few who can translate runes is one of the many old women who figure in the text, Mrs Evans, who is a witch. Runes, like Welsh, are the preserve of old women and reinforce their role as the keepers of tradition. Still, the Welsh language appears to be washed away with the flooding of the old Aberystwyth. Ultimately, these novels do not hold out much optimism for the fate of the Welsh language in a regenerated Wales.

House-proud and extravagantly religious, Mrs Llantrisant and her fellow members of the Sweet Jesus League Against Turpitude seem to represent a comic version of the Welsh mam. Louie explains that, '[h]er mother had swabbed this step and so had her mother and her mother before that. There had probably been a Mrs Llantrisant covered in woad soaping the menhirs in the iron-age hill fort south of the town'(4). Naming after place is not uncommon in this novel – Moulin girl Bianca's real name is later revealed as Sioned Penmaenmawr – but the surnames of the old women of Aberystwyth hint at their antiquity; like their place-names, they are as old as the hills. Despite her apparent foolishness, Mrs Llantrisant is eventually exposed as the fearless freedom fighter, Gwenno Guevara. When she is confronted by Louie with this revelation, he describes how 'a change came over Mrs Llantrisant. As if she had decided to drop the mask....The silly, frivolous old gossip faded away and in its place sat a different woman. Self-possessed and steely with an expression of stone.' (206) From this revelatory moment, Mrs Llantrisant is no longer 'a hunched and bent old spinster but who now walk[s] with a back ramrod straight and an authoritative purposeful air' (218). Foul-mouthed and murderous, a worthy opponent for Dai Brainbocs, it is Mrs Llantrisant who unleashes the bomb that is responsible for the flooding of the old Aberystwyth.

This performance and unmasking of cultural stereotypes has similarities with the way in which minstrelsy, formerly a cultural mode used to mock black people, has been appropriated by African-American artists and writers themselves. The American artist, Betye Saar, for example, uses many images of black stereotypes in her work in order to reclaim and reconstruct black identity. Her assemblage, *The Liberation of Aunt Jemima* (1972),[32] depicts the traditional black mammy figure of the white imagination carrying a gun. In this way, Saar shifts Aunt Jemima, originally a stock figure from nineteenth-century minstrel shows, from an obedient 'mammy' to one who threatens the white imagination. A similar challenging appropriation is seen in Barbara Neely's crime fiction, where her central investigative figure, Blanche White, is a subversive rendition of the traditional black mammy.[33] A domestic like Mrs Llantrisant, Blanche has a 'double consciousness';[34] her outwardly servile and foolish mask conceals her intelligence and rebellious nature. These minstrel manipulations disrupt the coloniser's infantilising and belittling images and endow them with a retaliatory power. Behind the blackface performance of the mammy or foolish old Welsh woman lies a lethal killer. Like the Aberystwyth tea-cosy shops in the harbour which act as a front for brothels, so the town and its inhabitants display a double consciousness; beneath the familiar, unthreatening surface lurks a dangerous presence.

Place

Hardboiled crime fiction is invariably married to a specific place; the father of the genre, Chandler, used Los Angeles as a setting, a tradition carried on today by James Ellroy. Even those hardboiled crime writers who have deliberately chosen a zero-setting often use features of their home towns as a template. Bill James has said of his *Harpur and Iles* novels that they are set in 'a nowhere place, about a nowhere situation'[35] but to the native reader, traces of James's Cardiff can be found within his work. Openly or covertly, then, contemporary crime fiction continues in its search for cultural identity.

In Pryce's novels, though, much of the comedy derives from the slippage between their genre and their setting. To the English visitor, Aberystwyth is a quiet seaside town, one not normally associated with the mean streets of hardboiled fiction. Occasionally, this place, like its inhabitants, appears to perform in blackface. Louie describes a drive to Borth as 'like sailing a ship over an ocean of grass as the road went up and down over the hills and dales. Every hillside was chequer-boarded with cows'(58-9). The Welsh countryside is laid out like a child's toy farm. Louie's portrayal of rural Aberystwyth initially seems nostalgic, childlike and comforting.

Nostalgia adds to the sense of a timeless Wales. Pryce's Aberystwyth also interweaves other versions of the town to create an anachronistic place, one that seems out of joint with contemporary life. As mentioned previously, this has much in common with the timeless Wales of Fforde and Leonard. While the opening line of the novel makes clear that it is set in the 1980s, mobile phones co-exist with witches and sedan chairs. The décor of Louie's office, 'a pre-war fan with bakelite knobs; a desk lamp from the Fifties; a modern phone and an answering machine'(6), is representative of the narrative's combination of early hardboiled tropes with contemporary motifs. Louie assures the reader that the styling is not 'deliberate and ironic'(6). Nevertheless, this cannot be held true of the prose. The view from Louie's office looks out 'across the slate roofs of downtown Aberystwyth towards the iron-age hill fort in

Pen Dinas: and beyond that to the four chimneys of the rock factory, now belching out pink smoke'(6). The landscape encompasses a hardboiled 'downtown', a physical reminder of Wales's pre-historic mythic past – a landscape often used in Welsh tourist merchandise – and a surreal depiction of industrialisation more reminiscent of a scene by the Welsh writer, Roald Dahl. Wales's prehistoric pagan past has been a favourite trope for English writers from Shakespeare's *Cymbeline* (1611)[36] to William Godwin's *Imogen* (1784)[37] to the work of eighteenth-century Romantic travel writers. However, Aberystwyth often displays a darker, Gothic face; Niall Griffiths, for instance, habitually portrays the more sinister aspects of this part of rural Wales. This is also explored in his non-fiction, *Real Aberystwyth* (2008),[38] which suggests an alternative to Tourist Wales. Aberystwyth may not be on a par with the mean streets of Los Angeles but neither is it simply the rural idyll of English imagination. Pryce's blending of the actual geography of Aberystwyth with differing imagined Waleses, including an infusion of 'mean streets', pokes fun at preconceived perceptions of place. Furthermore, the accompanying hardboiled murder rate of fictional Aberystwyth unsettles previously palatable images. The appropriation of American 'mean streets' is comic but also suggests an alternative to a constructed rural Wales, one which has something in common with Griffiths's gritty rural-*noir*.

Pryce's Tourist Aberystwyth contains many comic Gothic elements. One of its attractions is a surreal but authentic ghost train that is haunted by the unquiet spirits of tourists from the Midlands killed in an accident during its previous incarnation as an educational theme ride. Amongst its ghosts is a woman 'carrying a head under its arm with peroxide blonde hair'(99). It may seem as if Aberystwyth is haunted by its role as a holiday town. However, this figure has appeared before in the poetry of R.S. Thomas where her '[b]lue eyes and Birmingham yellow/Hair, and the ritual murder of vowels'[39] are an encroaching threat to Welsh identity. Thomas's poetry frequently alludes to the threat posed by English modernity to an ancient Welsh rural culture. Pryce kills off this threat and, during Louie and Myfanwy's visit to the ghost train at least, her presence fails to materialise. In this way, Pryce tries to shake off obsolete cultural stereotypes that align Welsh identity with a pastoral tradition.[40] Nevertheless, the idea of a Wales haunted by an English presence continues to exert a pull on the imagination as the supposedly authentic ghost train now attracts a new 'breed of visitor'(99).

Still, it is questionable why anyone would want to visit Pryce's Tourist Aberystwyth, for it is such an uncongenial spot. It is described as a frontier land, one that is inhospitable and rain-swept. On considering the inhabitants of a caravan park, Louie wonders, '[h]ow many other people had made the same journey as the rain swept in from the sea and pounded on the plywood roof of their shoebox on wheels? Families who had driven for two or three hours, stopping occasionally for puking children, to this world of gorse and marram grass, dunes and bingo and fish and chips'(151). Like the wagon trains that travelled West, the tourists in their caravans travel to mid-West Wales and show true grit in their determination to holiday in a place; while this nods towards one of hardboiled's progenitors, the Western, it also hints that this Aberystwyth has more in common with the Wild West pioneer towns of the past than the image packaged for the tourist market. For this is a lawless town, too, where the police are corrupt and can 'arrange for you to fall down the police station steps'(33) and where the Druids can orchestrate a person's disappearance. Pryce's Aberystwyth certainly contradicts the statement by David Williams's publishers that Wales, a picturesque haven, is a place in which crime does not occur.

Still, it is uncertain who wields the state authority in this novel. Set in a pre-devolution Wales, yet written after the setting up of the Welsh Assembly, the novel's Aberystwyth appears to be part of an independent, self-contained nation state. Most of this series centres on a local, hermetic setting, a common theme in Welsh appropriations of the hardboiled novel, as Welsh crime writers use the local to examine cultural identity in their fiction. Pryce takes this further as he imagines a self-sufficient nation. Swansea is its cosmopolitan centre, Llanelli Technical college provides cutting-edge technology such as the 'micro-dot photo booth'(136), Blaenau Ffestiniog is noted for its vineyards (161), and Gwent is home to Wales's perfumiers. Those fleeing Aberystwyth travel to Shrewsbury, which is situated on the border with England, a reversal of the author's own journey from Shrewsbury to Aberystwyth. The Ghost Train displays a sign asking '[w]hat is the purpose of your journey to England?', a question presumably asked at the Wales-England passport control. Nevertheless, this is a 'once-lovely' (237) town that has experienced a 'sad, slow fall from grace'(13). There are many references to a past Victorian or Edwardian splendour, a past that was outward-looking, almost imperialist in tone; Louie's 'great-great-uncle Noel Bartholomew'(7) had travelled to Borneo's heart of darkness to rescue an Englishwoman but, most significantly, the nation-state wages war in a far-flung outpost of its Empire, Patagonia.[41]

The fictional Patagonian Wars, 'the Welsh Vietnam'(94) featured in *Aberystwyth Mon Amour,* points to a Wales with a strong imperial past. While the Patagonian Wars are fictional, the settlement is, of course, based in reality. Settled by Welsh immigrants in the mid-nineteenth century as an effort to preserve Welsh identity from the corrosive influence of the English language, Y Wladfa [The Colony] has a hybrid identity which expresses itself through Welsh and Spanish. As Pryce avoids the use of English paradigms through his marriage of American hardboiled and Welsh tradition, so the Patagonian settlers effectively avoided

English cultural imperialism. Still, the Patagonian Wars of *Aberystwyth Mon Amour* also hint at the loss of Welsh life in Britain's Falklands Wars, a dispute over a similarly inhospitable and distant territory. Like the Falklands conflict, the patriotic and jingoistic mood surrounding the Patagonian Wars changed from 'initial euphoria. And then the disillusionment. The body bags and policy U-turns; the sobering discovery that the boys weren't the men in white hats as everybody had supposed'(94). In Patagonia, as in the Falklands, those who died, died for a '[f]igment of empire, whore's honour'.[42]

Beyond Aberystwyth, in its 'mountainous hinterland', lies the Forestry Commission plantation and Nant-y-Moch reservoir. This is a gloomy Gothic locality made up of 'sad unenchanted forests of conifers planted in uniform rows by the Forestry Commission'(101). Although a colonial imposition, the plantation and reservoir are indicative of Erdman's 'cultural identity', albeit an identity forged through resistance. Rooted in reality, both forest and reservoir are felt by some to be symbolic of the power a distant government had over the people of Wales and became the pivotal point in politicising groups such as Plaid Cymru. Formed in 1919, the Forestry Commission was established in order to break Britain's reliance on timber imports.[43] In later years it was given the power of compulsory purchase of Welsh farmland. Nant-y-Moch reservoir was constructed a year prior to the flooding of another village, Tryweryn. Although the flooding of Nant-y-Moch village does not seem to have incurred the protest that the flooding of Tryweryn did, today there is objection to the imposition of a wind farm by a Scottish power company. In this case the imposition does not entail the relocation of a Welsh village against their will, but it certainly continues the lack of consideration of a local voice by an outside agency. Matthew Jarvis recognises the role that forests and reservoirs, or in his words, 'wood and water', play in 'the destruction of communities and of the material structures on which those communities depended.' He goes on to describe this, memorably, as 'the politics of environmental disenfranchisement'; despite the comedic mode of Pryce's novel, there is a distinct air of such 'environmental disenfranchisement' in its depiction of 'sad' and 'unenchanted' expanses of 'wood[s] and water'.[44]

Lovespoon's plot to breach the dam's defences is pivotal to the narrative of *Aberystwyth Mon Amour*. Initially, Lovespoon's actions to take 'his people back' (86) to Cantref-y-Gwaelod can be read as a warning against the dangers of looking to a mythic past, especially when it is revealed that Lovespoon is English. The Chief Wizard, leading the town into danger, is a fake; his role as a bard and Welsh teacher is a performance of an English idea of Welshness. However, rather than reading his actions as a deluded and deadly attempt to return the people of Aberystwyth to Cantref-y-Gwaelod by flooding the town in a biblical deluge, Lovespoon's actions can be interpreted as returning Nant-y-Moch to the people of Aberystwyth, a metaphorical return of the villages and farmlands which were taken from the people of Wales by the Forestry Commission and water companies. Louie and Llunos's complicity in letting this happen, despite having the power to avert the bombing of the reservoir, seems to suggest this.

The final chapter sees Louie and Calamity emerge from a showing of a film depicting the flooding of the old Aberystwyth, possibly a reference to the 1949 Emlyn Williams film, *The Last Days of Dolwyn*,[45] a melodrama that featured the writer as a villain who plans to flood his home village as an act of revenge. In spite of Calamity's description of it as 'rubbish', Louie knows that secretly they both 'loved it'(239-40). Emlyn Williams has frequently been accused of staging a colonial performance in his writing. M. Wynn Thomas takes him to task for perpetuating the portrayal of a Welsh 'Uncle Tom'[46] in his play, *The Corn is Green* (1938). Louie and Calamity's ambivalence about the film certainly reflects the colonised's double vision, whereby the pleasure derived from a depiction of one's own culture competes with the knowledge that this is a stereotyped, blackface performance of that culture. Despite the film's melodrama and triumphalism, it is a story which continues to be shared with the people of Aberystwyth. A modern version of Cantref-y-Gwaelod, *Aberystwyth Mon Amour* celebrates the continuation of Welsh myth in shaping national identity.

The Solitary Gumshoe

Louie Knight, the central investigative figure, appears to escape the performance of minstrelsy. Louie, a native of Aberystwyth, displays none of the overblown grotesque characterisation that is typical of the druids or old women of the novel. In contrast to many of Aberystwyth's inhabitants: Myfanwy, Llunos, Mrs Llantrisant, whose Welsh names are indicative of their cultural identity, Louie is shaped through his performance of a hardboiled American P.I. This is the subject of much ironic comment within the text. On Louie refusing a glass of wine, Lovespoon comments, 'I was under the impression that hard-boiled private eyes were constrained by the requirements of stereotype to drink on every possible occasion'(161). Louie does drink, though in his case it is rum rather than the usual whisky, but it is ice-cream, 'a double with extra ripple'(11), that he turns to in moments of crisis. Reminiscent of childhood, 'a vanilla-soaked ticket back to where pain was just a grazed knee and a mother's caring hand was never far away' (12), it could be argued that the image of the P.I. with an ice-cream cone is another manifestation of the infantilised Other. However, here it is the American stereotype that is subverted and made vulnerable, softened even, in order to take its place in the Aberystwyth community.

Dennis Porter reminds us of how the private eye is 'a solitary eye...a non-organisation man's eye, like the frontier scout's or the cowboy's; an eye that trusts no other; an eye that's licensed to look; and even by extrapolation, an eye for hire'.[47] True to the stereotype, Louie is a loner who exists outside everyday society. This P.I. is neither part of an elite class who restores the status quo through solving crime, like his Golden Age precursor, nor part of a tight-knit team, as in the modern police procedural. Louie is tolerated by the corrupt police force. While Detective Inspector Llunos dislikes 'having private operatives sniffing around his turf', the policeman and the P.I. share an 'uneasy truce'(27). However, although Louie does work outside accepted state authority, he does not work alone in this series. He is partnered in his investigations by Calamity Jane, a schoolgirl who dreams of becoming a 'gumshoe'(16). Whilst unusual in P.I. fiction, Louie and Calamity are not the only instance of a P.I. and girl partner. This is a partnership also explored by Kate Atkinson in *When Will There Be Good News?* (2009)[48] the third in a series featuring Jackson Brodie, private eye. This particular novel sees Brodie team up with Reggie, an orphaned, friendless, sixteen-year-old girl like Calamity, to investigate the disappearance of Reggie's employer. Like Pryce's Aberystwyth novels, Atkinson's crime fiction is written post-devolution, albeit a Scottish devolution. These partnerships are an act of appropriation that take aspects of an individualised, solitary cultural figure like the P.I. and make him part of a community. Both Brodie and Louie, solitary, jaded P.I.s, are recast as father figures to an orphaned younger generation. Louie's partnership with Calamity indicates that detection in Welsh crime fiction is not necessarily the solitary activity of the hardboiled novel, but often a communal task. Louie also later joins forces with the ousted Detective Inspector Llunos, an act only possible once Llunos is no longer a member of a corrupt state authority. Together, in a moment of 'telepathy' and 'shared vision'(244), they allow the criminal act of flooding the town, one which leads to rebirth and new prosperity. Louie and Llunos's late friendship inhabits a grey area, or interstitial space that undermines accepted forms of authority. Rather than an individualised American culture which swamps the existing native culture, the P.I. is made Welsh. Detection is now a communal activity that works for the benefit of the community.

Conclusion

The reborn and regenerated Aberystwyth at the close of the text looks to Europe rather than hardboiled America and indicates a slippage in mimicry of Anglo-American culture. This is a new and prosperous Aberystwyth which has emerged phoenix-like, not from fire, but from water. Sospan's ice-cream kiosk is now a pavement café selling 'espressos and ristrettos'(240), while Sospan himself runs a chain of bistros and receives European Union funding. Written before the crash of the so-called Celtic Tiger, rather than this being an indication of Wales's further loss of identity, it mirrors independent Ireland's economic growth through the aid of European funding and points to an alternative to the Westminster government. The subsequently regenerated Aberystwyth is seen as an improvement for, as Louie remarks, '[p]rogress isn't always a bad thing'(240). Swept away by the flood is the figure of Noddy that had graced Sospan's ice-cream stand; this regenerated Aberystwyth no longer performs a minstrel version of itself and '[c]artoon characters had no place illuminating the espressos and ristrettos of Sospan's terrace café'(240). The regenerated town is one which no longer needs to replicate itself through the colonising gaze but looks outwards, secure in its own devolved identity, but now towards Europe rather than America. In truth, except for the ghostly traces of Bianca in her stovepipe hat, there are few traces of a Welsh culture in the regenerated Aberystwyth. But Pryce's Aberystwyth is one that suggests the possibilities of new hybrid, contemporary identities and avoids the 'cringingly colonial performance' that is 'stage-Welsh'.

NOTES

1 Stephen Knight, 'Crimes Domestic and Crimes Colonial: The Role of Crime Fiction in Developing Postcolonial Consciousness', in *Postcolonial Postmortems: Crime Fiction from a Transcultural Perspective* eds Christine Matzke and Susanne Mühleisen (Amsterdam and New York: Rodopi, 2006), pp. 17-34 (p. 31).

2 In an interview with the *New Welsh Review*, Lesley Grant-Adamson relates how she was told by publishers that 'Wales doesn't sell'. (Jackie Aplin, 'Making a Killing-Unless it's Welsh', *New Welsh Review*, 14 (Autumn 1991), 18-21 (p. 21)). Katherine John, speaking at *Criminal Intent*: *Crime Writing Conference for the Valleys* on 14th November 2009, also confirmed that she was discouraged from using her native Wales as a setting for her crime fiction.

3 Barry Forshaw, 'Last Tango in Aberystwyth by Malcolm Pryce', *The Independent* 13 October 2003, p. 12.

4 Jane Aaron and Chris Williams, 'Preface', in *Postcolonial Wales* (Cardiff: University of Wales Press, 2005), pp. xv-xix (p. xv-i).

5 During this time, the Welsh crime writer John Williams, whose work is published by Bloomsbury, also worked as an editor at Serpent's Tail. He must take some credit for the increased presence of Welsh crime fiction at these publishing houses.

6 Eva Erdman, 'Nationality International: Detective Fiction in the Late Twentieth Century', in *Investigating Identities: Questions of Identity in Contemporary International Crime Fiction* eds Marieke Krajenbrink and Kate M.Quinn (Amsterdam and New York: Rodopi, 2009), pp. 11-26 (p. 19).

7 Glyn Daniel's *The Cambridge Murders* (1945) and C. E. Vulliamy's *Don Amongst the Dead Men* (1952).

8 John Ellis Williams's *Murder at the Eisteddfod* (1973). This is a translation and reworking of his earlier Welsh-language novel *Y Gadair Wag* (1958).

9 David Williams's Mark Treasure series, the first of which is *Unholy Writ* (1976).

10 Raymond Chandler, 'The Simple Art of Murder' (1950). Available at http://www.en.utexas.edu/amlit/amlitprivate/scans/chandlerart.html (accessed 25 June 2010).

11 *The Oxford English Dictionary* defines the word as '[h]ardened, callous; hard-headed, shrewd' and dates its first usage to 1886.

12 Dylan Thomas, 'Old Garbo', in *Portrait of the Artist as a Young Dog* (London: Dent, 1940), pp. 183-210.

13 Gwyn Thomas, 'Oscar', in *The Dark Philosophers* (1946, Cardigan: Parthian, 2006), pp. 3-101.

14 Victor Golightly, 'Gwyn Thomas's American "Oscar"', in *New Welsh Review* 22 (Autumn 1993) 26-31 (p. 27).

15 Ed Thomas, *House of America, in Three Plays* (Bridgend: Seren, 1994), pp. 13-100.

16 Ed Thomas, 'The Welsh: A Land Fit for Heroes. (Max Boyce Excluded)', *The Observer*, 20 July 1997, p. 18.

17 My initial research has pinpointed Bill James's *You'd Better Believe It* (1985) as the moment that Welsh crime writers turn to the hardboiled mode in their fiction.

18 Chandler, op. cit.

19 Bernard Knight, *Tiger at Bay* (London: Robert Hale and Co., 1970), p. 1.

20 Bill Ashcroft, Gareth Griffiths and Helen Tiffin, *The Empire Writes Back: Theory and practice in post-colonial literatures* (London and New York: Routledge, 1989), p. 38.

21 Malcolm Pryce, *Aberystwyth Mon Amour* (London: Bloomsbury, 2001), p. 33. All further references are to this edition and are given in parentheses in the text.

22 Louie explains how the 'folk tale version told how the kingdom lying in the lowland to the west had been protected

from the sea by dykes and during a feast one night someone had left the sluice gates open. Similar stories were found all round the coast of Britain and seemed to be a folk memory of the land that was lost with the rising seas following the last ice age.' (p. 85)

23 The title of Alain Resnais' 1959 film, with a screenplay by Marguerite Duras, which is generally considered to have initiated the French *nouvelle vague*.

24 James Anderson, *The Affair of the Blood-stained Egg Cosy* (London: Constable, 1975).

25 Jasper Fforde, *The Eyre Affair* (London: Hodder and Stoughton, 2001).

26 Gaynor Madoc Leonard, *The Carmarthen Underground* (Talybont: Y Lolfa, 2009).

27 Clare Morgan, '*Aberystwyth Mon Amour* by Malcolm Pryce', in *The Times Literary Supplement*, 22 June 2001, p. 23.

28 A.A. Gill, 'A Rare Bite Worth Going to Wales for', *The Sunday Times*, 31 October 1993.

29 Jeffrey Green, 'Minstrelsy' in *The Oxford Companion to Black British History* eds David Dabydeen, John Gilmore, and Cecily Jones (Oxford: Oxford University Press, 2007), pp. 299-301 (p. 299).

30 Homi K. Bhabha, *The Location of Culture* (London and New York: Routledge, 1994), p. 88.

31 Amplified cartoon figures are a common device in cinema. From the animated Marshmallow Man of *Ghostbusters* (1984) to the giant Gingerbread man of *Shrek 2* (2004), the increase in scale is both comic and unsettling.

32 Betye Saar, *The Liberation of Aunt Jemima* (1972), Collection of University of California, Berkeley Art Museum.

33 Lee Horsley, *Twentieth-Century Crime Fiction* (Oxford: Oxford University Press, 2005), p. 235.

34 Horsley, p. 238.

35 Julian Earwaker and Kathleen Becker, *Scene of the Crime: A Guide to the Landscapes of British Detective Fiction* (London: Aurum Press, 2002), p. 80.

36 William Shakespeare, *Cymbeline, in The Norton Shakespeare* ed. Stephen Greenblatt (New York and London: Norton, 1997).

37 William Godwin, *Imogen: a Pastoral Romance, from the Ancient British* (New York: New York Public Library, 1963).

38 Niall Griffiths, *Real Aberystwyth* (Bridgend: Seren, 2008).

39 R.S. Thomas, 'Border Blues', in *R.S. Thomas* (London: J.M. Dent, 1996), pp. 36-39 (p. 36).

40 Pryce later satirises R.S. Thomas's so-called peasant poems in the third in the Aberystwyth series, *The Unbearable Lightness of Being in Aberystwyth* (2005). In this novel, one of the attractions is a Iago Prytherch Tourist Trail.

41 Pryce's *From Aberystwyth with Love* (2009) also includes a Welsh outpost, the little known town of Hughesovka, situated in what is now modern day Ukraine. Founded by nineteenth-century industrialist John Hughes, the town was the result of capitalist endeavour rather than a wish to escape English cultural imperialism. Nonetheless, the town contained a thriving Welsh community until the Russian revolution.

42 Tony Conran, 'Elegy for the Welsh Dead, in The Falklands Islands, 1982', in *Twentieth Century Anglo-Welsh Poetry,* ed. Dannie Abse (Bridgend: Seren, 2004), pp. 153-4 (p. 154).

43 'The Forestry Commission', in *The Encyclopaedia of Wales,* eds John Davies, Nigel Jenkins, Menna Baines, Peredur Lynch (Cardiff: University of Wales Press, 2008), p. 298.

44 Matthew Jarvis, *Welsh Environments in Contemporary Poetry* (Cardiff: University of Wales Press, 2008), p. 30.

45 *Last Days of Dolwyn*, dir. Russell Lloyd, Emlyn Williams (De Grunwald Productions, 1949).

46 M.Wynn Thomas, 'Flintshire and the regional weather forecast', in *Internal Difference* (Cardiff: University of Wales Press, 1992), pp. 68-81 (p. 73).

47 Dennis Porter, 'The private eye', in *The Cambridge Companion to Crime Fiction,ß* ed. Martin Priestman (Cambridge: Cambridge University Press, 2003), pp. 95-114 (p. 95).

48 Kate Atkinson, *When Will There Be Good News* (London: Black Swan, 2008).

Iago Prytherch's Mangels: Agricultural Contexts for R. S. Thomas's 'A Peasant'

Matthew Jarvis
University of Wales Trinity Saint David

In his poem 'A Peasant', from the 1946 volume *The Stones of the Field*, R. S. Thomas famously has his hill-farmer, Iago Prytherch, engaged in 'Docking mangels'; he is also described as ploughing (he 'churn[s] the crude earth') and as 'pen[ning] a few sheep in a gap of cloud'.[1] In my book, *Welsh Environments in Contemporary Poetry*, I have taken Prytherch's mangels (alternatively known as mangel-wurzels or mangolds, a root crop used as a feed for animals) to be an indicator of a greater fertility in the environment imagined by the poem than its opening rhetoric of 'bald Welsh hills' would imply. In short, I have suggested that it is important that '*something* has been growing here'.[2] On these terms, Prytherch's ploughing and his mangels can be seen as significantly connected, with the Welsh hill-farmer preparing the ground that he subsequently crops, whilst the poem specifically shows him 'Docking' the root crop after it has been harvested. However, Tony Brown has raised the question of whether the hill-farms of Wales are not too harsh for the growing of crops[3] – the potential for such growth, of course, being the basic premise for my reading of Prytherch's mangels as indicative of at-least-partial fertility in the poem's environment. It is Tony Brown's question that the main part of this primarily contextual essay seeks to address, whilst a shorter second section suggests that Iago Prytherch's mangels are not, actually, mangels at all. A brief concluding discussion considers the significance of such agricultural contexts for the sort of literary analysis undertaken by ecocriticism – that critical approach which foregrounds environmental issues in the discussion of literary/cultural objects and out of which tradition this brief study in part emerges.

*

R. S. Thomas's Prytherch draws on the experience of hill-farming in 1940s Montgomeryshire where R. S. had a parish (in the east of the county, in the village of Manafon) between 1942 and 1954. Writing to Raymond Garlick in March 1969 and recalling what might be called his ur-Prytherch moment, Thomas stated that 'The first poem I wrote about him – A Peasant – certainly was written in the evening after visiting a 1000'-up farm in Manafon where I saw a labourer docking swedes in the cold, grey air of a November afternoon'.[4] As others have observed, Thomas's Prytherch is thus not rooted in the valley village of Manafon – although Manafon is itself about 440 feet above sea-level – but in the hills that rise above it in the surrounding area.[5] The hills in the immediate vicinity of Manafon, to both the east and the west, reach around 800 to 1,200 feet in height. Moving six or seven miles to the west of the village, the higher hill-tops reach 1,400 or 1,500 feet, whilst Garreg-hir, seven-and-a-half miles west-south-west of Manafon, rises to nearly 1,600 feet. The sort of farming area from which the Prytherch figure emerges is thus precisely the sort of animal-raising hill-farm that, in their 1944 volume *The Agriculture of Wales and Monmouthshire*, A. W. Ashby and I. L. Evans classify as 'Cattle and Sheep (Poor Land)' – the topography of such farms being what they call 'an intermediate region' which is to be found 'Between the lowlands and the mountains', and which 'accounts for a considerable proportion of the farming area of Wales'.[6]

Ashby and Evans's study is especially important because its assessment of Welsh 'Types of Farming' (Chapter IX) draws on data about Welsh agriculture from 'the ten years 1929–30 to 1938–9'[7] – in other words, from the ten years immediately prior to Thomas's engagement with the

Montgomeryshire hill-farms and his writing of 'A Peasant'. It is a book which thus provides an invaluable picture of the state of Welsh farming in the years just before Prytherch's genesis. What is crucial for my purposes here is Ashby and Evans's description of Welsh hill-farms at the end of the 1930s. Their outline of the physical layout of such farms casts some useful initial light onto the material environment out of which the Prytherch figure was imagined:

> The typical homestead was built for shelter in the upper reaches of a valley, though some are in more exposed positions. Surrounding the house and buildings, a number of enclosed fields form the cultivated area of permanent pasture with a little arable. Beyond these, enclosed fields of poor pastures (*ffridd*) usually lead to the rough hill grazings proper. These are unenclosed, save for boundary walls or fences, though in some districts they remain as open hill over which a number of farms enjoy grazing rights in common.[8]

Of more immediate importance to the question of Prytherch's mangels, however, Ashby and Evans note that these farms – with an average of 60% of their land-area taken up by 'rough grazings' – put 'a little over one-twentieth' of their land-area to 'tillage crops'. Describing what these crops were, Ashby and Evans write:

> By the nineteen-thirties, oats was virtually the only cereal crop. Potatoes were grown on a small scale for domestic consumption, but the principal root and green crops were turnips, swedes and rape ....[10]

In other words, even though Ashby and Evans concede that such crops 'did not amount to very much', the sort of farmland from which the Prytherch figure emerged would, as a matter of course, have contained at least some 'tillage crops'. Indeed, a sense of the amount of land actually involved in the 5% of total land-area that was given over to 'tillage crops' on farms of this type is given by Ashby and Evans's observation that the average size of a Welsh hill-farm in this period was around 280 acres.[11] Admittedly, Ashby and Evans do not mention mangels as a hill-farm crop here. However, in discussing 'Cattle and Sheep (Better Land)' – their second Welsh farming type, consisting of lower-lying animal-raising farmland – they note that 'tillage crops' on such 'Better Land' were represented by 'less rape and a higher proportion of mangolds' than on 'the poorer land farms'.[12] In other words, mangels were to be found on the hill-farms too; they just did not make up as large a proportion of the overall cropped area as was the case with lower-lying farms. Moreover, writing in his 1948 book *Root Crops* (another volume usefully contemporaneous with the period of Prytherch's genesis), H. I. Moore makes the pertinent general point that root crops grown for animal fodder were, at this time, 'consumed on the premises';[13] in short, they were typically grown and consumed on the same farm. It is, I would suggest, precisely within these various contexts of land-use and agricultural procedure that we should understand Prytherch's mangels.

Of course, having moved to Manafon in 1942, Thomas's ur-Prytherch moment would have taken place during WW2. This was a period which had a profound impact on agriculture in the United Kingdom, not least because of the plough-up campaign, which – as Brian Short, Charles Watkins, William Foot and Phil Kinsman explain in their book *The National Farm Survey, 1941–1943: State Surveillance and the Countryside in England and Wales in the Second World War* – saw the conversion of considerable areas of grassland to arable in order to maximise food production.[14] As such, the agricultural situation in Britain developed rapidly in the period immediately following the years detailed by Ashby and Evans. Interestingly, in its attempt to increase 'emergency fertility', the WW2 plough-up campaign 'extended into rough grazings and elevations even above the 1300 ft contour'.[15] Moreover, whilst for 1940 (the first season of plough-up) the new arable land 'was to be sown with wheat where feasible, or otherwise with potatoes, oats, barley, beans, peas, rye or mixed corn', in 1941 the growth of 'roots for animal feed' was also encouraged.[16] It is thus not surprising that, whilst the emphasis of the plough-up campaign was very definitely on the production of food for human consumption,[17] the acreage put over to fodder crops also increased markedly. For example, in 1939, 216,000 acres of UK farmland were used for growing mangels; by 1945, that figure had grown to 308,000 acres.[18] In addition, the influence of the plough-up campaign was particularly marked in Wales, with 64% of all holdings in 1940 and 69% in 1941 reporting some land ploughed up – contrasting with 31% and 35% of English holdings, respectively, for the same years.[19] Indeed, a notable example of plough-up in Wales was, precisely, in Montgomeryshire – the 'Dolfor scheme',[20] which was photographed by Geoff Charles.[21] As such, by comparison with the situation of 1929–39 detailed by Ashby and Evans, wartime Wales had seen a notable increase in land used for 'tillage crops', even stretching into 'areas on the boundaries of viable cultivation'.[22] Admittedly, as the *Summary Report* of the 1941–43 National Farm Survey of England and Wales indicates, what was still the 'comparatively small tillage area' of tough upland farms was more than two-thirds dedicated to fodder crops.[23] But such comments make unambiguously clear that the 1940s farmland of Prytherch's conceptual genesis was certainly not land on which crops were not grown.

*

Two further points about Prytherch's mangels might also usefully be addressed here: the twin questions of 'Docking' and of what precisely is being docked. To *dock* something is to take part of it away. More technically, it is a term used to describe the process of reducing the length of an animal's tail.[24] In this sense, the word suggests the removal of an extremity. In his 1948 volume *Root Crops* that I mentioned above, H. I. Moore observes that swedes, for example, are prepared for storage by being 'topped and tailed'[25] – a process which fits the notion of 'Docking' very neatly. As Henry Stephens explains in his mid-nineteenth-century text *The Book of the Farm*,[26] topping and tailing involves slicing off both the leafy green matter at the top of the plant and the thin, trailing root at the bottom, leaving the main part of the root (the bulbous 'storage organ') trimmed in the middle.[27] The extremities, in other words, are removed. However, as H. I. Moore also notes:

> In contrast to the treatment of swedes, the tops [of mangels] are usually screwed off by hand and the roots are not trimmed. When topping-knives are used the tops are not severed close to the crown. Care is taken also on most farms to avoid injury to the roots, which are, therefore, thrown into carts by hand instead of using forks.[28]

Indeed, a British government advisory leaflet from the 1970s makes a similar point when it indicates that 'Mangels bleed easily so the leaves are cut above the crown, or twisted off when crops are lifted before full maturity'.[29] Significantly, such accounts of the careful treatment that mangels require do not sound much like what Prytherch is doing. Rather, Thomas's accompanying description has Prytherch 'chipping the green skin/From the yellow bones' – a process which suggests that, if skin is being chipped off, the root is definitely being damaged, with its underlying, hard flesh (the 'yellow bones') thus being exposed.

Of course, Prytherch may just be being insufficiently careful with the mangel crop; as Henry Stephens indicates in *The Book of the Farm*, 'slicing off a portion, and hacking the skin of the bulb [the storage organ], indicates carelessness'.[30] But another issue suggests that Prytherch may not actually be dealing with mangels anyway. This is the fact that mangels are not green skinned. Mangel skin 'can vary from red, orange and yellow to white',[31] yet Thomas explicitly has Prytherch removing 'green skin'. However, in recalling his ur-Prytherch moment, it was swedes that Thomas remembered being docked. Unlike mangels, swedes can have green skin – and are typically yellow-fleshed – all of which is congruent with the image of green skin being taken off the bone-like yellow hardness of the root itself.[32] As such, we might propose that Prytherch's mangels are not actually mangels and that they are, in fact, swedes. Such a proposition would, moreover, fit with Ashby and Evans's note that the main root crops of Welsh upland farms in the 1930s were turnips *and swedes*, and – as another fodder crop – would not conflict with the upland emphasis on growing roots for animal feed that was identified in the *Summary Report* of the 1941–43 National Farm Survey of England and Wales.

In short, it seems that, in 'A Peasant', R. S. Thomas has Iago Prytherch 'Docking mangels' notwithstanding a subsequent description which suggests that Prytherch is dealing with a different root-crop entirely. Perhaps Thomas was drawn to this particular word by the rhythmic shape it offered to the line ('Docking mangels' permits the line to open with two trochees, which is far more rhythmically fluent than the alternative 'Docking swedes'); perhaps mangels sounded more exotic than swedes, thus echoing something of the grandeur implicit in Prytherch's own name which, suggesting the Welsh form *ap Rhydderch*, marks him as a descendent of Welsh princes (albeit, in some way, simultaneously a Iago-like betrayer of that heritage);[33] or perhaps R. S. was simply not so much of a countryman himself at the point of writing this poem, and was unaware of – or was poetically unconcerned by – such fine-grained agricultural distinctions. Whatever speculations one might advance in this respect, however, one point does seem clear: that Iago Prytherch's mangels in 'A Peasant' are not mangels at all.

*

Such factual issues seem to matter a great deal to ecocriticism – that environmentally-centred approach to literary/cultural analysis out of which, as my introductory remarks indicated, this essay partly emerges. In the words of Lawrence Buell, perhaps its leading American proponent, ecocriticism has displayed 'a preoccupation with questions of factical accuracy of environmental representation'.[34] However, such a preoccupation has, according to Buell, 'given rise to considerable anxiety and division' within ecocritical ranks 'at a time when privileging literature's capacity for mimesis and referentiality remains unfashionable'.[35] Indeed, Buell's analysis suggests that the notion of mimesis has proven to be particularly divisive, with 'mimesis police'[36] – those ecocritics he describes as having 'scrupulously absorbed' the 'anti-mimetic' tendencies of 'the (post)structural revolution'[37] – set against 'neo-realists', whose approach has been to prioritise 'texts and genres that seemed to provide dense, accurate representations of actual natural environments'.[38] As I have argued elsewhere, I have no desire to deny the capacity of literature to be a linguistic/discursive response to what Kate Soper calls 'extra-discursive reality' and thus to have some form of referential or mimetic capacity;[39] nor, however, do I wish to suggest that what appears in the literary text is (or, worse, *should be*) some simple reflection of such 'extra-discursive reality'. Rather, I have proposed that:

> as a discursive response to the physical world, the text constitutes an active engagement with that world in the sense that the linguistic act offers a *judgement* upon the

> world, a judgement on how that world (or, at least, the part of it under consideration) should be seen, understood, or conceptually approached. Rather than being reduced to a process of mimicry – which will always, of necessity, be entirely partial – each act of writing the environment is, at its core, an argument about how the world should be seen: it is nothing less than an invitation to understand, to approach the world in a particular way ....[40]

R. S. Thomas's 'bald Welsh hills' in 'A Peasant' are just such an invitation to see the world in a particular way; more specifically, of course, they are an invitation to see *Wales* in a particular way. They are also congruent with a significant strand of bleak/bare environmental imagery which runs through a good deal of Thomas's early work – a tendency, however, that is crucially in dialogue with a counterbalancing sense of non-human richness. For example, and merely to draw on work in *The Stones of the Field*, the 'Country Child' will discover how 'the world will grow to a few lean acres of grass' even as 'An ash tree wantons with sensuous body and smooth'.[41] 'Man and Tree' observes the 'gnarled hand' of the tree on the similarly 'meagre shoulder' of the man, yet both are seen as more effective teachers in their 'old silence than in youthful song'.[42] Likewise, 'The Airy Tomb' offers up a 'cold country',[43] a 'gaunt wilderness', a 'lean patch of land',[44] yet simultaneously contends that this is a place where 'grass and tree/Are a green heritage more rich and rare/Than a queen's emerald or an untouched maid'.[45]

The contextualising work of the main part of this essay, with its suggestion that the 'extra-discursive reality' of upland farming areas in 1940s Montgomeryshire lies at some distance from Thomas's opening environmental rhetoric in 'A Peasant' (those 'bald Welsh hills'), is in no way intended to criticise the poet for some sort of departure from the extra-textual world. Rather, it seeks to offer up the necessary cultural/historical/environmental information to reveal that Thomas's 'A Peasant' is engaged in a very clear process of environmental construction – one which the poem, through its imagery of Prytherch's root-crop, also emphatically undercuts. In this sense, 'A Peasant' manifestly displays that environmental double-vision which I have just suggested is identifiable elsewhere in Thomas's early work. Indeed, whilst my remarks above about the mangels themselves speculated on possible *reasons* for their appearance in the poem, precisely, as mangels rather than as swedes, the *effects* of such naming undoubtedly play into this complex environmental dynamic: specifically, the poem's vision of the 'Poor Land' hill-farm on which the poet situates Iago Prytherch is overlaid with the image of a root-crop which, according to Ashby and Evans (as I noted earlier), is more typically associated with lower-lying 'Better Land'.[46] Simultaneously, however, it should further be observed that, whilst mangels might generally point towards a notion of better Welsh farming land, their description ('the green skin', 'the yellow bones') – *literally* indicative of swedes, as I have argued – *figuratively* plays into the notion of a Welsh environment which is gaunt, lean, and little more than a decaying corpse. In short, 'A Peasant' is environmentally shifting terrain, catching very precisely the complex doubleness of R. S. Thomas's early poetic response to the non-human world. The work with which this essay has been primarily concerned – that of providing environmental contexts for a literary object – is thus not designed to chastise a writer for some presumed departure from the extra-textual matter of what Lawrence Buell calls 'the palpable world'.[47] Rather, the sort of spade-work I have undertaken here is, I would contend, a fundamental part of that process by which criticism may unearth the potential richness of the literary-environmental act itself.

NOTES

My thanks are variously due to Professor Tony Brown of the R. S. Thomas Study Centre at Bangor University for raising the question that prompted this essay; to Dr. Philip Colbourn, subject librarian for agriculture at Aberystwyth University, for comments and suggestions which have been incorporated into the text; and to Dr. David Green, formerly lecturer in agricultural economics at Aberystwyth University, for general advice on farming questions. I am grateful to the estate of R. S. Thomas for permission to quote from the poetry of R. S. Thomas (© Kunjana Thomas 2001): 'A Peasant', 'Country Child', 'Man and Tree', and 'The Airy Tomb' from R. S. Thomas, *The Stones of the Field* (Carmarthen: Druid Press, 1946).

1 R. S. Thomas, *The Stones of the Field* (Carmarthen: Druid Press, 1946), p. 14.

2 Matthew Jarvis, *Welsh Environments in Contemporary Poetry* (Cardiff: University of Wales Press, 2008), p. 24.

3 Personal discussion.

4 R. S. Thomas, *Letters to Raymond Garlick 1951-1999*, ed. Jason Walford Davies (Llandysul: Gomer, 2009), p. 75.

5 See, for example, Brian Morris, 'The Topography of R. S. Thomas', in Sandra Anstey, ed., *Critical Writings on R. S. Thomas* (Bridgend, UK: Seren, 1992), pp. 112-27: p. 116. In discussing the originating area of 'the composite figure of Prytherch', Morris is, however, wrong to assert that 'the hills and moorland of Cefn Coch above Adfa' are 'more than ten miles to the West' of Manafon: as the crow flies, Cefn Coch is four miles from Manafon. Nor, as he asserts, does Mynydd y Gribin – some two-and-a-quarter miles to the west of Cefn Coch – 'rise to over 1500 feet'.

6 A. W. Ashby and I. L. Evans, *The Agriculture of Wales and Monmouthshire* (Cardiff: Gwasg Prifysgol Cymru; [London]: Honourable Society of Cymmrodorion, 1944), p. 101.

7 Ibid., p. 100.

8 Ibid., p. 101.

9 For the rudimentary state of the farms themselves in this period, see Edith H. Whetham, *The Agrarian History of England and Wales,* vol. 8 (Cambridge: Cambridge University Press, 1978), p. 197. Ashby and Evans, *Agriculture,* p. 101.

10 Ibid.

11 Ibid. It may also be useful to see such figures in the context of root-crop production which, according to Ashby and Evans, for the period 1929-38 in Wales, saw turnips and swedes cropping at 11.8 tons per acre and mangels cropping at 16.6 tons per acre (ibid., p. 26).

12 Ibid., p. 103.

13 H. I. Moore, *Root Crops* (London: Farmer & Stock-Breeder; London: Spon, 1948), p. 108.

14 'More than 4.25 million acres [were...] ploughed up in the first two seasons' of the plough-up campaign (1940 and 1941); this amounted to around 20% of 'the pasture area in June 1939': Brian Short, Charles Watkins, William Foot and Phil Kinsman, *The National Farm Survey, 1941–1943: State Surveillance and the Countryside in England and Wales in the Second World War* (Wallingford: CABI, 2000), pp. 34 and 33.

15 Ibid., p. 34.

16 Ibid., pp. 33 and 34.

17 Ibid., p. 32.

18 Ibid., p. 36.

19 Ibid., pp. 218 and 217.

20 Ibid., p. 218.

21 Geoff Charles (1909–2002) was a key photographer of twentieth-century Welsh life, and 'Some of his images have become iconic': see John Davies, Nigel Jenkins, Menna Baines and Peredur I. Lynch, eds, *The Welsh Academy Encyclopaedia of Wales* (Cardiff: University of Wales Press, 2008), p. 136. Charles's photographs are held by the National Library of Wales. For an online archive of his wartime material, including his images of the Dolfor scheme, see National Library of Wales, *Geoff Charles: Photographs of Wales and the English Border During the Second World War,*

<http://geoffcharles.llgc.org.uk/home.php>, 24 July, 2010.

22 Short et al., *State Surveillance*, p. 218.

23 Great Britain, Ministry of Agriculture and Fisheries, *National Farm Survey of England and Wales (1941-1943): A Summary Report* (London: HMSO, 1946), p. 80.

24 See *Oxford English Dictionary*, 2nd edn, entry for 'dock *v.*[1]', definitions 2a and 1b.

25 Moore, *Root Crops*, p. 91.

26 Henry Stephens, *The Book of the Farm*, 2nd edn (Edinburgh: Blackwood, 1855), vol. 1., pp. 192–3.

27 The term 'storage organ' refers to the various 'specialized structures at or below the soil surface' which root crops use 'to store starches and sugars': see Stephen K. O'Hair, 'Root and Tuber Crops', in Charles J. Arntzen, ed., *Encyclopedia of Agricultural Science* (San Diego: Academic, 1994), vol. 3, pp. 637–45: p. 637.

28 Moore, *Root Crops*, p. 92.

29 Great Britain, Ministry of Agriculture, Fisheries and Food, Agricultural Development and Advisory Service, *Fodder Root Crops*, Advisory Leaflet 591, amended ed. (Pinner: Ministry of Agriculture, Fisheries and Food, 1975) p. 8.

30 Stephens, *Book of the Farm*, p. 193.

31 Agricultural Development and Advisory Service, *Fodder Root Crops,* p. 3.

32 For skin and flesh-colour of swede varieties, see Moore, *Root Crops*, p. 8.

33 For the significance of the name *Rhydderch* in Welsh royal history – and *ap Rhydderch* indicating the line of descent – see David Walker, 'Caradog ap Gruffudd ap Rhydderch (*d.* 1081)', *Oxford Dictionary of National Biography,* <http://www.oxforddnb.com/view/article/48539>, 6 Aug., 2009.

34 Lawrence Buell, *The Future of Environmental Criticism: Environmental Crisis and Literary Imagination* (Oxford: Blackwell, 2005), p. 31.

35 Ibid.

36 Ibid., p. 40.
37 Ibid., p. 31.
38 Ibid., pp. 32, and 40.
39 Kate Soper, *What is Nature? Culture, Politics and the Non-Human* (Oxford: Blackwell, 1995), p. 8.
40 Jarvis, *Welsh Environments*, pp. 10–11.
41 Thomas, *Stones,* p. 16.
42 Ibid., p. 19.
43 Ibid., p. 42.
44 Ibid., p. 43.
45 Ibid., p. 42.
46 Ashby and Evans, *Agriculture,* pp. 101 and 102–3.
47 Buell, *Future of Environmental Criticism*, p. 33.

The Value of Official Records to Studies of R. S. Thomas's Life and Writings

Sheila Savill
Independent Scholar

Introduction

R. S. Thomas's mother, orphaned at six and subsequently 'sent' away to an English boarding school, had few memories of her parents. Thomas's father was away at sea for much of the poet's childhood. Subsequently, communication between them became inhibited by his father's loss of hearing. For those reasons, R. S. Thomas [henceforward R.S.] said, he knew little about his ancestors and that little was 'almost entirely hearsay'.[1]

This essay, based on recent research in official records, suggests that (as commonly happens with family stories) such 'hearsay' as R.S. passed on to enquirers was a mixture of accurate, inaccurate and misleading information. It seeks, also, to demonstrate that the hitherto untapped material in official records, such as the Register of Births, Marriages and Deaths [BMD], Census Returns, and the *National Probate Calendar*, extends and deepens our understanding and appreciation of R.S.'s life and writings.

For reasons of space, the focus will be on evidence concerned with R.S.'s mother and her relatives, but official records also contain previously undiscovered information about his father and paternal family. For example, it seems that R.S. believed, and others have unquestioningly followed his belief, that his father, Thomas Hubert Thomas, was the 'the eldest son ... sent to sea in 1898, aged sixteen ... to help support his widowed mother', and her large, young family.[2] However, the 1901 Census Return for Cardiff shows that Thomas Hubert, then 17, was the third son and fourth child of his parents' eight children.[3] His father, James Thomas, was still alive, and working as a coal merchant. When James died, on the 24 April 1907,[4] Thomas Hubert was 23, and all his younger siblings old enough to support themselves. There appear to have been no grounds for R.S.'s belief that major responsibilities fell upon his father's shoulders.[5]

Turning to the story of the poet's mother, we find an example of what will be shown to be strictly accurate, though initially puzzling and misleading, information: R.S. said on different occasions that his orphaned mother, Margaret, had been brought up by 'an aunt and her husband, who was a parish priest'; and 'by a half brother who was a vicar'.[6] The solution to this apparent contradiction will emerge, together with other new information, from the following discussion of official documents concerning Margaret and her family.

Margaret Davies and her family

1912. Marriage solemnized at St Mark's Church in the parish of Gabalfa in the County of Glamorgan

No.	When Married.	Name and Surname.	Age.	Condition.	Rank or Profession.	Residence at the time of Marriage.	Father's Name and Surname.	Rank or Profession of Father.
137	Oct 8th 1912	Thomas Hubert Thomas	28	Bachelor	First Mate	167 Whitchurch Road Cardiff	James Thomas (Deceased)	Cashier
		Margaret Davies	21	Spinster	—	Clive House Inglefield Avenue Cardiff	Llewelyn Davies Deceased	Cashier

Married in the Church of St Mark according to the Rites and Ceremonies of the Established Church by Licence by me, R. B. Evans Vicar

This Marriage was solemnized between us, Thomas Hubert Thomas, Margaret Davies. In the Presence of us, Elizabeth Jones, William John Jones.

Fig I. Marriage certificate of Margaret Davies and Thomas Hubert Thomas (detail)

395	Twenty ninth March 1913 5 Newfoundland Road Gabalfa Llandaff RD	Ronald	Boy	Thomas Hubert Thomas	Margaret Thomas formerly Davies	Commercial Traveller Oils and Grease	T. H. Thomas Father 5 Newfoundland Road Gabalfa Llandaff	Ninth May 1913	[illegible] Registrar	

Fig 2. Birth Certificate of Ronald [R.S.] Thomas (detail)

Taken together, these two certificates are illuminating. They also raise several questions. First, the wedding, held on 8 October 1912, was conducted 'by licence', not 'after banns', which take some four weeks to be called.[7] This suggests that it may have been (not, necessarily, that it was) a hastily-arranged affair. The date on R.S.'s birth certificate, 29 March 1913, gives a possible reason for haste:[8] Margaret must have been some three months pregnant when she married. Here, therefore, is the probable basis of R.S.'s repeated suggestion that his mother trapped Thomas Hubert into marriage:

> ...She went fishing in him;
> I was the bait
> That became cargo...[9]

A comparison of the certificates also shows that there were some grounds for R.S.'s suggestions, for example in the poem 'Salt', that his mother lured his father away from the sea, for, although he was a First Mate when he married, by the following May, when he registered his son's birth, Thomas Hubert had become a 'Commercial Traveller Oils and Grease'.[10] Here, therefore, we have the origin of that image R.S. employs so effectively in *The Echoes Return Slow* to suggest a sluggish life, in a disgusting, polluted environment:

> ...the young couple,
> choosing the capital of a fake
> nation to be their home; the father travelling in
> 'oils and grease' in between rougher surfaces of the
> ocean.[11]

The name of R.S.'s paternal grandfather, James Thomas, has long been known, and his character and antecedents are discussed in Byron Rogers' official biography,[12] but no previous reference has been found to the name of R.S.'s maternal grandfather, identified in the marriage certificate as Llewellyn Davies. His profession, 'cashier,' suggests humble origins and raises questions about how someone of this class came to be closely related to, possibly even the father – or stepfather – of an Anglican clergyman.

The prominence of Elizabeth and William John Jones as the wedding's official witnesses suggests that they were important members of the bride or groom's family. Was William Margaret's clerical half-brother/uncle, giving his half-sister/niece away in marriage, or was the officiating Vicar, R.W. Evans, that relative?

The Census Return of 1911 for Cardiff[13]

Some, though not all, of those questions can be answered from the information given in the 1911 Census return for the Jones's home in Cardiff, which describes Margaret as William Jones's sister-in-law and a member of his household. R.S. never seems to have mentioned his mother's having any sisters, but evidently she had at least one, Elizabeth Jones.

Elizabeth's husband, William, was not Margaret's clerical relative, for his 'employment or profession' is given in the Return as a 'Commercial Traveller Paper Manufacturers'. That incidentally suggests that perhaps William Jones had prompted, even possibly facilitated Thomas Thomas's change to shore-based work, as a commercial traveller, albeit in different commodities.

The return also tells us that Elizabeth was 15 years older than Margaret. Victorian families were notoriously large, but since R.S. refers to his mother having a half-brother, possibly Elizabeth was a half-sister. In order to clarify the relationship one would need to know whether the two women had the same or different fathers, a question that could be answered by finding the Joneses' own marriage certificate.

The Census Return includes the information that the Joneses had been married for 12 years and that, like Margaret herself, Elizabeth and all three of the Jones children, Ivy, Violet and Gwynne, had been born in Merthyr Tydfil.[13] It therefore seems probable that the Jones wedding would have been held in Merthyr in c.1899. However, all initial attempts to trace that certificate proved fruitless: many William John Joneses aged about twenty-two had married girls named Elizabeth in Merthyr, in or around 1899, and the only wedding of an Elizabeth Davies and William John Jones seemed almost certainly not the one being sought. While this tended to lend weight to the hypothesis that Margaret and Elizabeth had different fathers, until the name of Elizabeth's father was known for sure, progress here seemed unlikely. The search therefore turned to identifying Margaret's – and possibly – Elizabeth's mother.

Margaret Davies' Birth Certificate and the Census Return of 1891 for Merthyr Tydfil

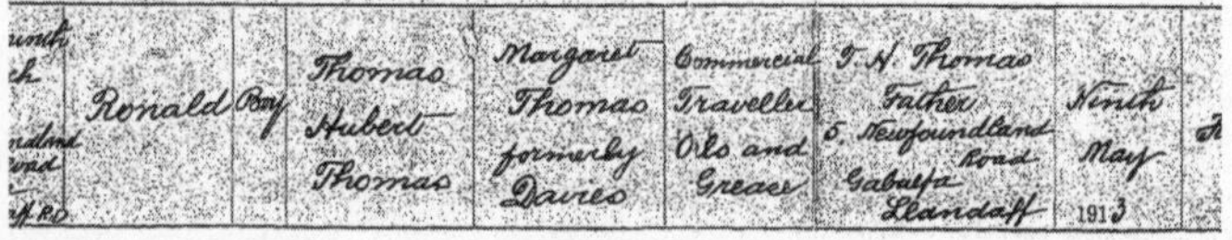

Ronald	Boy	Thomas Hubert Thomas	Margaret Thomas formerly Davies	Commercial Traveller Oils and Grease	T. H. Thomas Father 5, Newfoundland Road Gabalfa Llandaff	Ninth May 1913

Fig 3. The Birth certificate of Margaret Davies (detail)[14]

Margaret's father seems to have been a pedantically conscientious man, for her birth certificate shows that, when registering her arrival, he included unusually detailed – and very helpful –information about her mother, whose 'Name, surname and maiden name' he gave as, 'Elizabeth Davies late Jones formerly Roberts'. If Margaret had any half-siblings, therefore, some of them might have the surname of Jones, or Roberts.

The certificate (fig. 3) gives the Davies's address, 3

Windsor Place, Merthyr Vale, making it easy to find them in the 1891 census, which took place on 5 April.[15] There, Margaret's half-sister, 15-year-old Bessie Jones, is recorded as living with her mother, Elizabeth Davies, step-father Llewellyn Davies, and the infant, Margaret, whose age is given as 'four weeks'. (Though Margaret was in fact 3 weeks old, census enumerators commonly 'rounded up' infants' ages to the nearest month, so the small discrepancy is insignificant). As Elizabeth Davies's age is given as 39, she must have been born c.1852 and been about 24 when she had Bessie. Were there no surviving children between the two girls? Could Bessie Jones be identified, for sure, with Elizabeth Jones? Did she have an older brother? When had her father died and what was his Christian name? A new search for the Joneses' marriage certificate, begun on the assumption that Bessie and Elizabeth Jones could be the same person, brought success, and answers to several outstanding questions.

Fig. 4 The Marriage Certificate of Elizabeth Jones & William John Jones (detail)[16]

…age solemnized at the Parish Church in the Parish of Merthyr Tydfil in the County of …

Name and Surname.	Age.	Condition.	Rank or Profession.	Residence at the time of Marriage.	Father's Name and Surname.	Rank or …
Richard David	31.	Bachelor	Clerk in Holy Orders	Merthyr Tydfil	Evan David	[illegible]
[illegible] Jones	23	Spinster	—	[illegible]	Thomas Jones	[illegible]

… Church according to the Rites and Ceremonies of the Established Church, by Licence … by me,

… David / … Jones } in the Presence of us, { [illegible] / [illegible] — Daniel Lewis, Rector.

This certificate, dated 11 July 1898, shows Elizabeth's father to have been a 'publican' called Thomas Jones. The name and profession of William Jones's father are also recorded, as 'Isaac Jones, Minister', incidentally suggesting the possibility that the Jones family may have been those relatives in south Wales that R.S. said his mother 'greatly enjoyed visiting and being pampered by ... because she was an orphan,' although as a child he himself felt uncomfortable and disliked staying in their home, because 'They were Nonconformists, a bit Puritanical'.[17]

The 1901 Census for Merthyr Tydfil tells us that Isaac Jones was a minister of the Welsh Baptist church.[18] Some surprise has been expressed about the fact that the son of such a Minister married a publican's daughter; but we know that Elizabeth's father was long dead, her step-father seems to have been an eminently 'respectable' working man and, of course, not all Baptists will have been prejudiced.

Census Returns for Llanfabon and Merthyr Tydfil 1861, 1871, 1881

'Thomas Jones' is a very common name in Wales, 'Elizabeth Roberts' fairly common, too. Tracing Elizabeth's parents via Census Returns proved easier than finding them in BMD registers. The 1861 Return for the Llanfabon district of Merthyr includes an Elizabeth Roberts, aged 9 – the right age to be the same person as Bessie Jones and Margaret Davies's mother.[19]

Her parents were Henry, a Licensed Victualler, and Ann Roberts, of the Royal Oak, Glynrhynny, Llanfabon. She had three siblings, Evan, 19, Ann, 6, and Mary, 5. The 1871 Census Return[20] shows that the family had moved from Llanfabon to the Windsor Arms, Cardiff Road, Merthyr Vale. Elizabeth was no longer with them. However, she reappears in their household's record in the 1881 census,[21] now named Elizabeth Jones, and described as Henry Roberts' widowed daughter and accompanied by daughters of her own, Annie Jones, aged 12 and Elizabeth, 5. The age of the younger Elizabeth suggested she was the same person as the Bessie Jones of the 1891 census record and the Elizabeth who became the wife of William Jones.

Further searches of the 1871 Returns showed that Elizabeth and Thomas Jones, with their infant daughter, Annie, aged 2, had taken over the licence of the Old Oak in Llanfabon from Elizabeth's father, Henry Roberts. Elizabeth cannot have been more than 17 when Annie was born, her husband only a little older, for in 1871, he was twenty-three. His address and his 'employment or profession,' – given as 'coal miner and licensed victualler' – are additional confirmation that he was Elizabeth Jones' 'publican' father.

R.S.'s mother, therefore, had two half sisters, Annie, 22 years her senior, and Elizabeth (Bessie), 15 years older than she. It seems that there may have been a closer bond between Margaret and Elizabeth than between her and Annie, to whom no reference had previously been discovered.

Margaret's maternal grandparents were, also, now identified as Henry and Ann Roberts. However, no half brother had appeared. Had Elizabeth and Thomas Jones's marriage produced a surviving male child, he would, surely, in 1881, also have been living with his mother, or local relatives, but no such youth could be traced.

Margaret's maternal uncle, Evan Roberts, had died, in 1883,[22] so he could not be the clerical relative, who, according to R.S., had assumed responsibility for Margaret after her parents' deaths, nor could the cleric have been the husband of either of her two maternal aunts, for her mother's sister Ann remained unmarried and the husband of the other, Mary, was a mechanic, Isaac Brown.[23]

Fig 5. The Marriage Certificate of Elizabeth Jones & Llewellyn Davies (detail)

1898. Marriage solemnized at St. [illegible] Church in the [illegible] of [illegible] in the County of Glam[illegible]

No.	When Married.	Name and Surname.	Age.	Condition.	Rank or Profession.	Residence at the time of Marriage.	Father's Name and Surname.	Rank or P[illegible]
7	11 July 1898	William John Jones	22	Bachelor	Grocer	Merthyr Vale	Isaac Jones	[illegible]
		Elizabeth Jones	22	Spinster	—	Merthyr Vale	Thomas Jones	[illegible]

[M]arried in the Chapel of St. John according to the Rites and Ceremonies of the Established Church, by or after Banns

This Marriage was solemnized between us, William John Jones, Elizabeth Jones

in the Presence of us, Mary Jane Evans, Albert Richard Evans

Daniel Evans

The fact that Margaret's half-brother/uncle had not been identified with any member of the Roberts family suggested enquiries should be turned towards her paternal relatives. Her parents' marriage certificate (fig. 5) both confirms that Henry Roberts was indeed her maternal grandfather and gives her paternal grandfather's name as John Davies, his profession as 'Carrier,' validating the sense of Llewellyn's humble origins already obtained from Margaret's own wedding certificate.[24]

Information on the Davies family from the Census Returns of 1861 & 1871, for Llanwonno

The 1861 Return shows 'Llewelinn' Davies, aged 6, as the son of John and Ann Davies, of 'Household 98, Mountain Ash Village, Llanwonno'. He had an older sister, Ada, aged eight. Their father was employed as an agricultural labourer, at this period in the nineteenth century, the profession of some of the 'poorest of the poor'.[25]

By 1871, the family had moved to 17 Oxford Street Llanwonno. Llewellyn was now working as a coal wagon checker, his sister Ada as a 'general servant' and an older sister, who had apparently been away from home on the night of the previous census, 'Ellanor', aged 23, as a dressmaker.[26] No record of any marriage by an Ellanor or Eleanor Davies has been traced in the BMD indices. She may have died in 1878.[27] Llewellyn's other sister, Ada Davies, married William Lloyd, a plumber, in 1876.[28] It therefore seemed improbable that Margaret's clerical relative could be a member of her father's family. As he was said to have taken responsibility for her on the death of her parents, might their death certificates offer a clue to his identity?

The Death Certificates of Elizabeth & Llewellyn Davies

...1897 ... Place ... Vale	Elizabeth Davies	Female	45 years	Wife of Llewellyn Davies Colliery weigher	Morbus cordis Certified by J. C. Edwards L.R.C.P.	Ll. Davies Widower of Deceased Present at Death 3 Windsor Place Merthyr Vale	Fifteenth March 1897

Fig 6. Death Certificate of Elizabeth Davies (detail)[29]

Elizabeth's certificate shows that she died at home of heart failure on 14 March, 1897, the day before Margaret's sixth birthday. Her husband, who had been with her at the time, registered her death the next day. The only other names given are of officials, the doctor and registrar certifying her demise.

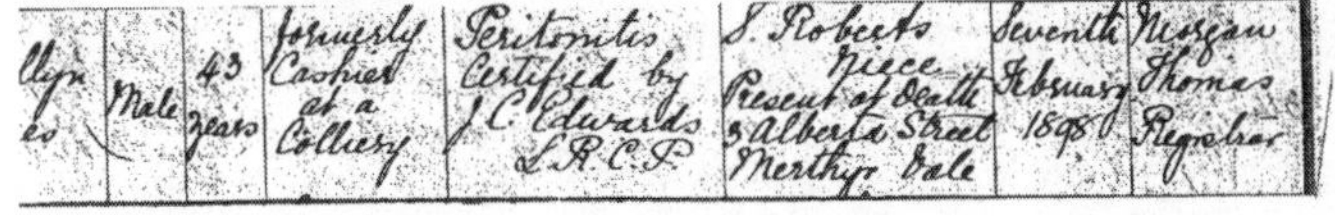

...llyn ...es	Male	43 years	formerly Cashier at a Colliery	Peritonitis Certified by J. C. Edwards L.R.C.P.	S. Roberts Niece Present at Death 3 Alberta Street Merthyr Vale	Seventh February 1898	Morgan Thomas Registrar

Fig.7 Death Certificate of Llewellyn Davies (detail)[30]

Llewellyn's certificate (fig. 10) records that he died less than a year later, on 6 February 1898, also at home. His end, from peritonitis, must have been protracted and agonising, very distressing to witness. It was registered the next day by an 'S. Roberts Niece', who had been with him at the end, and whose address was 3 Alberta Street, Merthyr Tydfil. Again, no one else, apart from officials, is named.

The 1901 Census Return for Merthyr Tydfil[31]

The 1901 Census Return for Merthyr Tydfil identifies 'S. Roberts' as Sarah Roberts. Checks in earlier census records of the Roberts family show her to have been the eighteen-year-old daughter of Elizabeth Davies's deceased brother, Evan. So far, it has been impossible to discover whether Margaret and Bessie were still living at 3 Windsor Place. If so, perhaps Bessie was caring for Margaret, and trying to shield her from knowledge of her father's agony. But why was their young cousin, Sarah, having to take on so much responsibility? Where were Llewellyn's sister, Ada Lloyd, his sisters-in-law, Ann Roberts and Mary Brown, his older step-daughter, Annie, and where was that clerical relative? Why were none of these people apparently involved in supporting the dying widower and his younger daughters? Official records do not offer clear answers to those questions. They do, however, suggest some possible ones.

Census Return 1891 and 1901 for Neath & the Returns of 1891 and 1901 for Merthyr Tydfil[32]

It seems possible that Llewellyn's sister, Ada, did not learn of his illness in time to be able to support him, for the Census Returns of 1891 and 1901 make it clear that she and her husband's home was in Neath.[33]

Further searches in the Merthyr Tydfil Census Returns showed that his step-daughter, Annie Jones, had continued to live with the maternal grandparents, Henry and Ann Roberts, and her Aunt Ann Roberts, Henry and Ann Roberts' second daughter, who remained unmarried. By 1891, Henry Roberts, now aged 76, was retired, and – at what date is unclear - he had moved with the three Anns of his household to an 'upmarket' address, Maesyffynon, in Treharris, a hamlet on the fringe of Merthyr Vale. That was still within easy reach of Windsor Place. However, early in the summer of 1891, soon after the census, Henry's wife died and searches through the Death Register's indices led to the record of his own death on 30 May 1898.[34]

Fig. 8 Death Certificate of Henry Roberts (detail)[35]

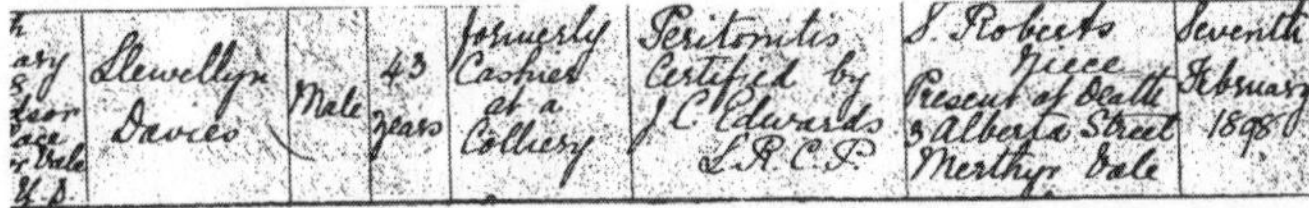

Llewellyn Davies	Male	43 years	formerly Cashier at a Colliery	Peritonitis Certified by J C Edwards L.R.C.P.	S. Roberts Niece Present at Death 3 Alberta Street Merthyr Vale	Seventh February 1898

This certificate gives the cause of Henry's demise as 'Paralysis. Exhaustion' so it seems likely that for weeks, possibly even months, as his end approached, he had needed more or less twenty-four hour care. The 1901 Census Return tells us the 37 household had two servants, a cook and a maid, but his middle-aged daughter, Ann, and his granddaughter, Annie, must have felt hard-pressed, Annie especially so, for she also had infant sons aged one and two to look after.[36] It would not, therefore, be surprising if they had felt unable to cope with the caring for Llewellyn, too, especially as peritonitis is apt to present as a sudden emergency, allowing no time for planning.

The probable psychological effects of repeated bereavement on the young Margaret Davies

Llewellyn Davies, Margaret's father, had died at the beginning of February, her grandfather at the end of May, 1898, so within little more than a year, and still only just seven, she had lost both parents and grandfather. In those circumstances, it must have felt like yet another major loss to her when, on 11 July, 1898, only 6 weeks after their grandfather's death, her sister Bessie left home to marry William John Jones.

The effect on so young a child of the repeated loss of her most significant adults must have been unimaginably traumatic. It explains Margaret Thomas, the adult's, attempts to keep her husband safely at home in shore-based work, her following him 'from port to port', during

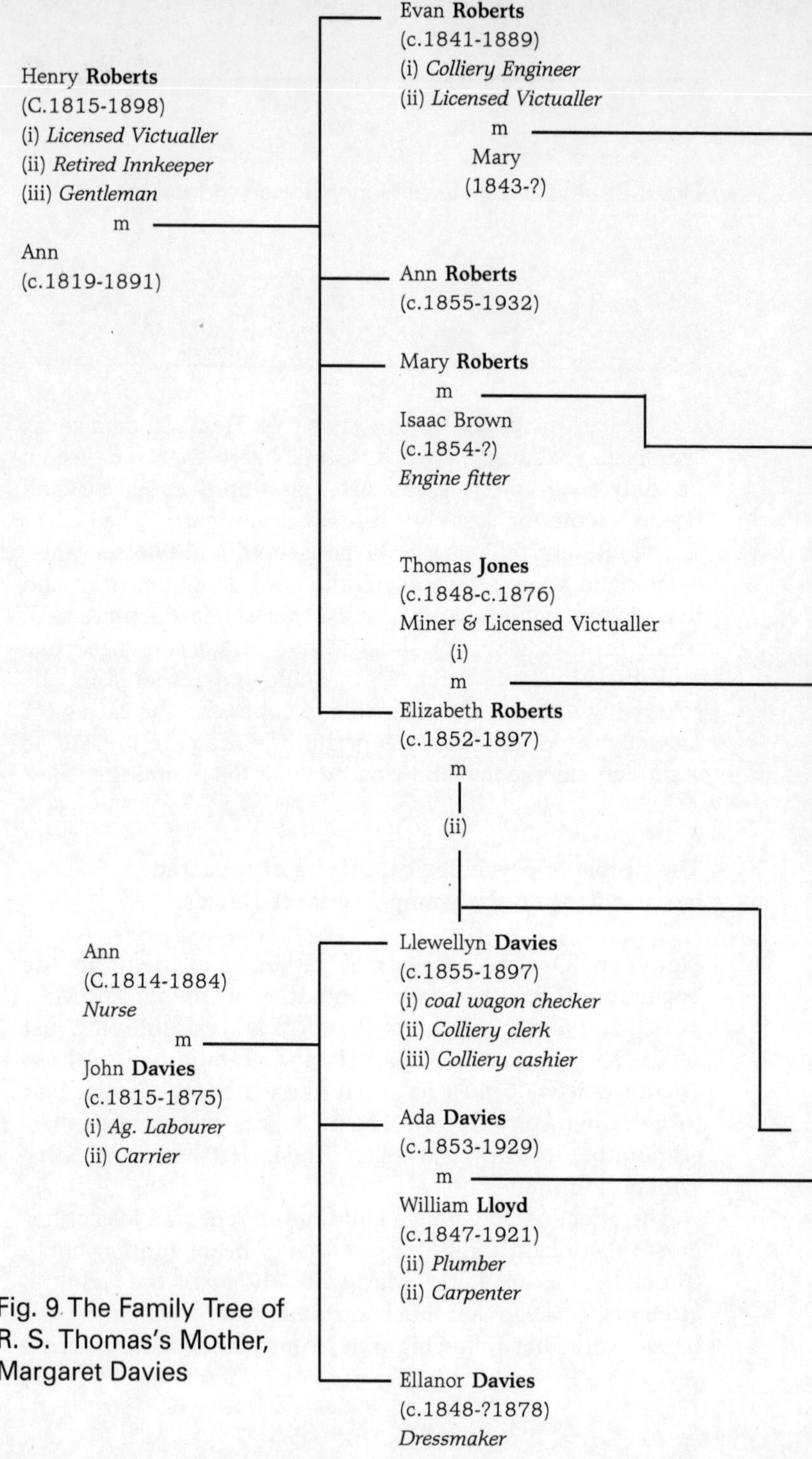
Henry **Roberts**
(C.1815-1898)
(i) *Licensed Victualler*
(ii) *Retired Innkeeper*
(iii) *Gentleman*
m
Ann
(c.1819-1891)
Evan **Roberts**
(c.1841-1889)
(i) *Colliery Engineer*
(ii) *Licensed Victualler*
m
Mary
(1843-?)
Ann **Roberts**
(c.1855-1932)
Mary **Roberts**
m
Isaac Brown
(c.1854-?)
Engine fitter
Thomas **Jones**
(c.1848-c.1876)
Miner & Licensed Victualler
(i)
m
Elizabeth **Roberts**
(c.1852-1897)
m
(ii)
Ann
(C.1814-1884)
Nurse
m
John **Davies**
(c.1815-1875)
(i) *Ag. Labourer*
(ii) *Carrier*
Llewellyn **Davies**
(c.1855-1897)
(i) *coal wagon checker*
(ii) *Colliery clerk*
(iii) *Colliery cashier*
Ada **Davies**
(c.1853-1929)
m
William **Lloyd**
(c.1847-1921)
(ii) *Plumber*
(ii) *Carpenter*
Ellanor **Davies**
(c.1848-?1878)
Dressmaker

Fig. 9 The Family Tree of R. S. Thomas's Mother, Margaret Davies

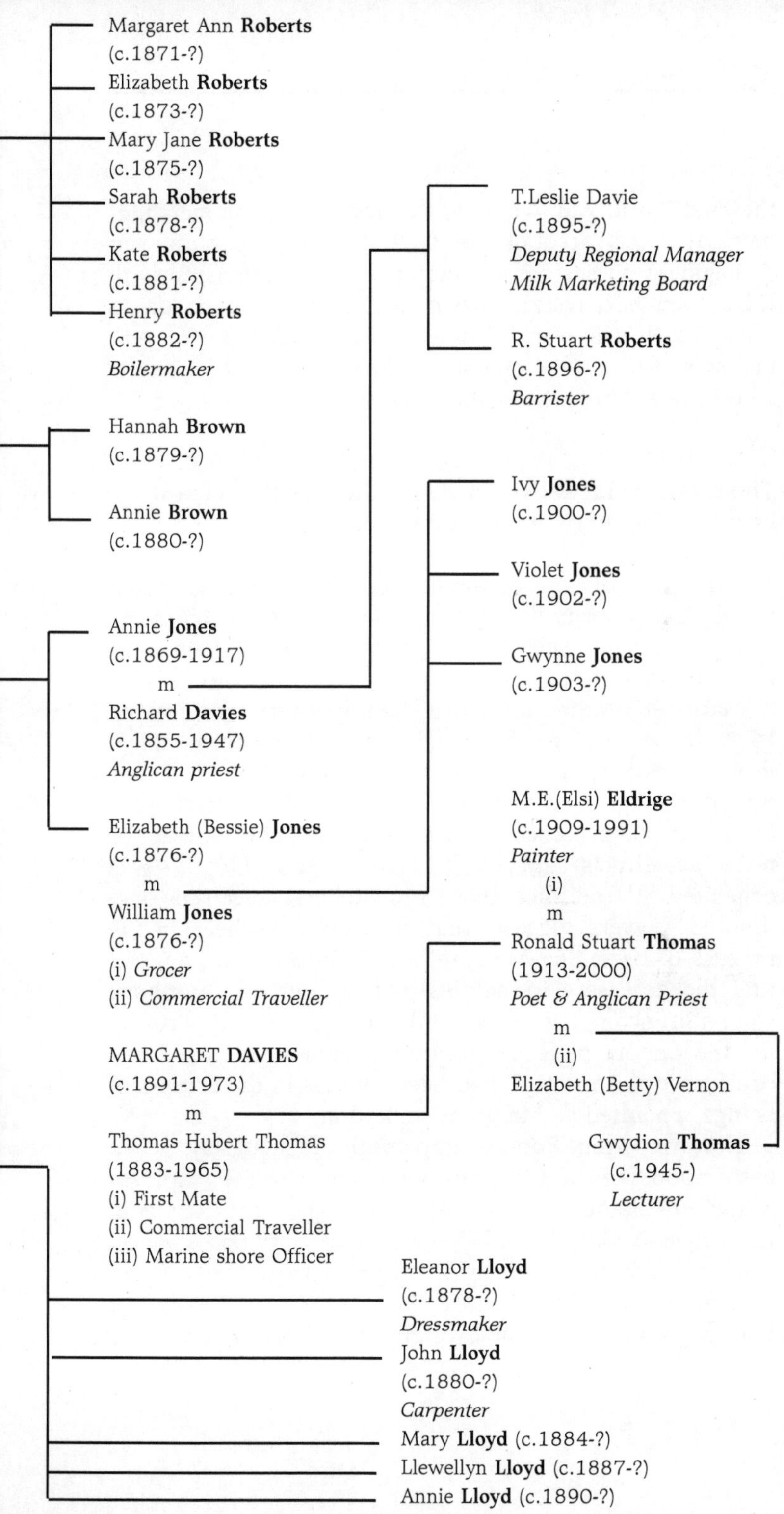
Margaret Ann Roberts
(c.1871-?)
Elizabeth Roberts
(c.1873-?)
Mary Jane Roberts
(c.1875-?)
Sarah Roberts
(c.1878-?)
Kate Roberts
(c.1881-?)
Henry Roberts
(c.1882-?)
Boilermaker
T.Leslie Davie
(c.1895-?)
Deputy Regional Manager
Milk Marketing Board
R. Stuart Roberts
(c.1896-?)
Barrister
Hannah Brown
(c.1879-?)
Annie Brown
(c.1880-?)
Ivy Jones
(c.1900-?)
Violet Jones
(c.1902-?)
Gwynne Jones
(c.1903-?)
Annie Jones
(c.1869-1917)
m
Richard Davies
(c.1855-1947)
Anglican priest
Elizabeth (Bessie) Jones
(c.1876-?)
m
William Jones
(c.1876-?)
(i) Grocer
(ii) Commercial Traveller
M.E.(Elsi) Eldrige
(c.1909-1991)
Painter
(i)
m
Ronald Stuart Thomas
(1913-2000)
Poet & Anglican Priest
m
(ii)
Elizabeth (Betty) Vernon
Gwydion Thomas
(c.1945-)
Lecturer
MARGARET DAVIES
(c.1891-1973)
m
Thomas Hubert Thomas
(1883-1965)
(i) First Mate
(ii) Commercial Traveller
(iii) Marine shore Officer
Eleanor Lloyd
(c.1878-?)
Dressmaker
John Lloyd
(c.1880-?)
Carpenter
Mary Lloyd (c.1884-?)
Llewellyn Lloyd (c.1887-?)
Annie Lloyd (c.1890-?)

the First World War, when he was recalled to the merchant navy. It surely accounts, as well, for the immature, and damagingly possessive, character of her relationship with R.S., even her hysteria when he left home to go up to university.[37] The work of Bowlby, Rutter, Winnicott, *et al.* has shown how characteristic such behaviour is of adults who have suffered traumatic loss as children.[38]

The estate of Llewellyn Davies & the question of who became Margaret's Appointed Guardian

The question of who became Margaret's official guardian during her minority has, as yet, no clear answer, but some evidence exists to suggest that her guardian may have been her aunt, Ann Roberts.

Margaret's father, Llewellyn, had died intestate, leaving £74. 4s. 1d. – a few thousand pounds in modern values. Probate records show that on 31 August 1898, Ann Roberts was granted 'limited' Letters of Administration for the estate. No evidence has been found to show whether or not Llewellyn's surviving sister, Ada Lloyd, was consulted.[39] The fact that Ann Roberts received only 'limited' powers suggests that she may have been in the process of becoming Margaret's Appointed Guardian, but that the necessary formalities in the Court of Guardians were still incomplete. It is improbable that her application for the Letters of Administration would even have been considered if Ann Lloyd had been, or was in the process of being, appointed as Margaret's guardian.

However, Ann Roberts apparently felt uneasy at an association with anyone of so humble a social status as Margaret's father. In the details she gave the Registrar, Llewellyn Davies, a colliery cashier of 3 Windsor Place, was transformed into Llewellyn Parry Davies, an accountant, of Clive Cottage, Windsor Place![40] This not only suggests the possible origins of Margaret Thomas's social sensitivities but, more importantly, offers a clue as to how, and why, she lost all contact, with and – given her age, probably all memory of – her Lloyd aunt, uncle and cousins (see Fig 9). That, in turn, could account for R. S.'s feeling that, certainly on his mother's side, he was virtually without relatives, 'not a family man'.[41]

The census of 1901 and the mystery of Margaret's whereabouts

R.S. said that his mother claimed that, after her parents' deaths, she had been 'sent to a boarding school in England' and 'deprived of love'. Byron Rogers quotes him as saying more specifically that Margaret had been despatched to a church school in Wantage.[42] The census of 1901 shows that there were several such schools in Wantage, and Margaret, now ten, might well have been thought old enough for boarding school, but is not recorded among the pupils in any of them, or as living elsewhere in the town.[43] Nor, indeed, can she be found anywhere in the United Kingdom at the time of that census, taken on 31 March.

Further research showed that both William and Elizabeth Jones are also missing from that census record; but their infant daughter, one-year old Ivy, is included: she was staying with her paternal grandparents, the Revd. Isaac and Mary Jones, at their home, Satem Villa, Ystradyfodwg,[44] leading one to ask whether Elizabeth and William were abroad, possibly in connection with his work as a commercial traveller for paper manufacturers, and had taken Margaret with them. This hypothesis is, to some extent, supported by the evidence, quoted earlier, that Elizabeth Jones, who had shared her parental home, remained close to, and caring towards, her much younger half-sister. The fact that ten years later Margaret was a member of the Joneses' household, as well as the couple's presence at Margaret's wedding, implies that William Jones supported his wife's concern for her. However, there seems to be no *evidence* as to what did happen to Margaret, or where she lived, between the death of her mother, in March 1897, and her appearance in the Joneses' household, in Cardiff, in 1911. Nonetheless, some evidence has now been found to put a name to the elusive clerical half-brother/uncle who, according to R.S., assumed responsibility for her after she had been orphaned.

The Curate of Merthyr Tydfil

Henry Roberts' death certificate (fig. 8) says his demise was registered by an 'R. David', of the same address, who had been present at the death; but it gives no further information about that person. A search of the 1901 Census Return for Merthyr Tydfil led to the discovery that the R. David living at Maesyffynon with Henry Roberts' family in 1898 had, by 1901, become the head of the Maesyffynon household. His full name is given as Richard David, his profession as 'Clergyman Church of England'. Aged forty-five, he was married to Margaret's half-sister Annie, now more formally named Ann (never again does any official document refer to her as Annie), thirteen years his junior.[45]

Here, at last, therefore, was Margaret's clerical relative, the Curate of Merthyr Tydfil, her half-brother, not by consanguinity, but by his marriage, in August 1892, to one of her half-sisters.[46] More or less the same age as her father, and her aunt, Ann Roberts, Richard David must have seemed to seven-year-old Margaret much more like an uncle than a brother. There may be another reason for the impression R.S. sometimes gave that the clerical relative was the husband, not of one of his own aunts, but, rather of one of Margaret's aunts.

Documentary evidence of a curious relationship

The 1901 Census Return tells us that Margaret and Annie's spinster aunt, Ann Roberts, was still living at Maesyffynon House. It has not so far been possible to establish whether she owned it, but under her father's will (see below), she had inherited all the household goods and furnishings, so it is a moot point as to whether she was living with the Davids or they with her, whether Richard David was the actual, or merely the titular, head of the household.[47] When, in 1912, Richard moved, with his wife, to take up the living of Llantwit Major, Ann Roberts accompanied them.

After Richard's wife died on 16 May 1917, he and Ann Roberts went on living together until she, too, died, on 11 November 1942, twenty-five years after her niece. Whether or not their relationship was, or ever had been, sexual, for everyday purposes this elderly couple were living like husband and wife, though they could not marry because, at that time, it was still illegal for a man to marry his deceased wife's aunt.[48] When, however, Richard David himself died, aged 91, on 1 September 1947, he was buried, presumably at his own request, in the single grave that already held the remains not only of his wife, Ann[ie], but also those of Ann Roberts – so, even in death, the trio were not divided.[49]

It is, of course, not unknown for self-consciously 'correct' manners, even prudery, to become the protective palimpsest of unconventional behaviour, but was R.S. possibly unfair to his uncle when he suggested that Margaret's upbringing had left her so inhibited that her husband's life also became constrained by the stifling conventions and mores of the (Victorian) vicarage:

> ...Was he aware
> of a vicarage garden
> that was the cramped harbour
> he came to?[50]

On a literal level, not until he was inducted into the living of Llantwit Major in 1912 – the year R.S.'s parents married – did Richard David acquire a vicarage, let alone a vicarage garden but, more importantly, the boundaries of his symbolic 'garden' to which R.S. seems to be alluding, appear, at least from one perspective, to have been unusually broad.

Richard David's clerical career: evidence from the Census Returns of 1881 and 1891

Richard David had ended his life as Vicar of Llantwit Major, Rural Dean of Groneath Lower and Canon of Llandaff Cathedral, a cleric of some eminence, whose funeral was conducted by his bishop.[51] His earlier career had been very different. Between 1887 and 1900 he was in his fourth post as a curate,[52] and before his marriage, in 1992, to the granddaughter of Henry Roberts, who was a wealthy man (see below), he seems to have been very hard-up indeed.

The 1891 Census Return for Merthyr Tydfil shows him lodging with an elderly labourer and his wife, not the kind of accommodation or social circle in which a Victorian clergyman was expected to make his home.[53] The 1881 Return for Upton-Upon-Severn gives him as unemployed, a 'curate without cure of souls', and pathetically ensuring that the enumerator also recorded that he was a BA.[54] (His landlord was a plumber and painter, leading one to speculate that, possibly, like some unemployed graduates today, Richard may have been earning his board and lodging by turning his hand to a spot of painting and decorating). Not until 1900, at the age of 44, did he at last attain the status of a vicar, and then only as Vicar of Treharris, the hamlet of which he was already a resident.[55]

Margaret Thomas will have been ignorant of these

inauspicious beginnings to the canon's career. Had she known them, she might not have so determinedly urged R.S. to follow him into the Anglican ministry.

A puzzling lack of evidence for Richard David's involvement in Margaret Davies' life

Initial consideration of Margaret and Thomas Hubert's marriage certificate left unanswered the question of whether R.W. Evans, the officiating clergyman, might have been her clerical half-brother/uncle. Plainly he was not; but nor can Richard David have 'given away' the bride, for if he had, he would have been recorded as an official witness to the marriage. Indeed, with a single exception, discussed below, no record has so far been discovered of Richard David's in any way involving himself in the care, welfare, or support of his young, traumatically orphaned sister-in-law. Nor has any evidence been discovered to show that Margaret ever lived with him and his family.

It seems, however, possible that he, his wife, and, presumably, Aunt Ann Roberts, did initially try to provide Margaret with a home; but the Davids' own children, Leslie (b. c.1896) and Stuart (c.1897), were still babies when she became orphaned. It is possible that, as happens with some traumatised children, she was so emotionally needy that she resented attention being given to the infants – may even have been aggressive towards them and, unable to cope, the Davids decided some other home must be found for her.

That is, of course, speculation, but it would account for the adult Margaret's complaints of having been 'deprived of love' and 'sent' to a boarding school. It is possible to understand her saying that her clerical half-brother/uncle had 'sent' her to boarding school as meaning he had paid for her education; but it seems much more likely that Margaret was using 'sent' rather in the sense of saying that the clergyman had 'got rid of', or 'banished' her to the school.[56] The fact that Richard David did not make himself financially responsible for her may add weight to that interpretation, although, since Richard, together with Ann Roberts, was responsible for managing her money (see below) the distinction is unlikely to have been apparent to Margaret until she was older.

Money for Margaret: information from Henry Roberts' Will

During her minority, the costs of Margaret's maintenance and education may have been paid partly by the money from her father Llewellyn's estate, but the primary source of funding was a substantial legacy from her maternal grandfather. The Will of 'Henry Roberts Gentleman' is dated 12 November 1897.[57] At his death the following May, the net value of his estate, according to the Probate record, was initially estimated to be £14,023. 2s. 5d., later revised to £15,844. 18s.1d.[58] It is difficult to be precise about how much that represents in modern terms, and different criteria would be applicable depending upon whether, for example, one is considering the relative power to buy the necessities of daily living, under the Retail Price Index, or the relative proportion of the Gross Domestic Product the historic sum would represent. (The reader is referred to the authoritative explanation of these criteria and their varying appropriateness to be found on the website of the Economic History Society at www.measuringworth.com). Different criteria produce widely varying results, but, to give the extremes, the present value of Henry Roberts' estate would lie between a minimum of £1,310,000 and a maximum of £13,000,000.[59] It included investments in the Merthyr coalfield and a great deal of property, both residential and commercial.

Margaret was left one eighth of the estate's property and one twelfth of its residue, with instructions that interest on the legacies could be used for her maintenance and education. At her trustees' discretion, the residuary capital could be transferred to her when she was 21 (i.e. in 1912, the year she married) and the capital of the principal legacy on, or after, her 30th birthday (March, 1921). The Will's executors and trustees, given responsibility for managing the whole of the estate, were Ann Roberts and Richard David, so they were also jointly responsible for handling Margaret's funds and for making the decisions as to when (and if) she received the capital. (Whether or not that capital was, eventually, made over to her, has eluded discovery).

The value of the legacies will of course, have depended on how competently, or otherwise, Ann Roberts and Richard David managed the capital, and possibly, to some extent on the value of property in the early years of the new century, but the Executors were instructed to sell the property and invest the proceeds, so any decline in property values during the years following Henry Roberts' death, would not necessarily have affected Margaret inheritance.

...a girl from the tip
Sheer coal dust
The blue in her veins.[60]

Henry's wealth, and the legacies Margaret received under his Will, suggest the substance behind R.S.'s jibe that that his mother's 'blue blood' came from the coal tip; but we now see it also implies his recognition that his grandfather was one of Merthyr's 'aristocracy'. Possibly there is also a hint that most blue blood has grubby origins, but that may be reading into his words something he did not intend to imply.

The Thomas family's finances

The fact that Margaret could afford, during the early years of her marriage, to follow her husband from port to port is probably accounted for by her inheritance. That, also, was a likely source of the funds that enabled R.S. to be sent to a private kindergarten and to take advantage of a grammar school education – an education many parents of his day could not afford for their children.[61] It is not, at present, clear whether the Thomases' house in Holyhead, in which they lived from 1919 until the end of their lives, was owned or rented by them. If they did own it, possibly some of Margaret's inheritance may have gone towards its purchase price, though such a contribution may have been unnecessary, as her husband was also a legatee under the will of his own grandfather, Edmund Thomas, a man three times as wealthy as Henry Roberts.[62]

Yet, by the time R.S. was contemplating university, his parents were short of funds.[63] It is impossible to tell whether this *volte face* was due primarily to the General Slump, was to some extent attributable to trustees' incompetence, or even in part to R.S.'s parents' not managing money very well. Byron Rogers quotes Gwydion Thomas's remarks about his father's horror of debt and the elderly Margaret and Thomas Hubert's regularly being visited by debt collectors. Possibly, therefore, all three factors played a part in their inconveniently reduced circumstances, as R.S. was growing up.[64]

Conclusions

This paper, based on research in nationally-held official records, suggests three conclusions:

- in matters of family history, independent verification of hearsay evidence should always be sought;
- official records contain valuable information that

extends and enhances our understanding and appreciation of R.S.'s life and writing;

- other official records, held more locally (and, therefore, inaccessible to the present writer) might well prove equally worth exploring. For example, parish records (usually found divided between county and diocesan archives) should reveal whether Richard David conducted his mother-in-law's and step-father-in-law's funerals, Margaret Davies's baptism, or indeed the baptism of R. S. Thomas. Land Registry documents would reveal the ownership of Maesyffynon House after Henry Roberts' death and whether or not R.S.'s parents owned their Holyhead home; local records of the Court of Guardians show who was in fact appointed as Margaret Davies's guardian.

guardian.O

NOTES

1 John Barnie & Ned Thomas, 'Probings', *Planet*, April/May 990, p. 28; R.S.Thomas ,'No-One', Autobiographies, (London, J.M. Dent 1997) pp. 34-35.

2 Byron Rogers, *The Man Who Went into the West* (London: Aurum Press Limited, 2006) p. 66;

3 Registrar General [in future abbreviated to R.G.] (1901) Census Return, Cardiff, RG13/4979/22.

4 R.G. (1907) Register of Deaths, 1907, Cardiff District, June Quarter, Vol. 11a, p.184.

5 R.S. Thomas, 'No-One', pp. 34-35.

6 R.S. Thomas, 'R.S. Thomas', Adele Sarkissian (ed.) *Contemporary Author Autobiography*, vol.4 (Detroit: Gale Research Company, 1986) p. 302.

7 R.G. (1912) Register of Marriages, 1912, Cardiff District, Dec. Quarter, Vol. 11a, p. 705. The designation of Thomas Hubert Thomas's father as a cashier is a clerical error of the type not uncommon in such certificates.

8 R.G.(1913) Register of Births, 1913, Cardiff District, June

Quarter, Vol. 11a, p. 697.

9 R. S. Thomas, 'The Boy's Tale', *Collected Poems* 1945-1990 (London: J.M. Dent, 1993) p. 142, ll. 17-19.

10 R. S. Thomas, 'Salt', *Collected Poems* 1845-1990 London: J.M. Dent, 1993) pp. 345-346.

11 R.S. Thomas, *The Echoes Return Slow*, (London: Macmillan, 1988) p. 4.

12 Byron Rogers, *The Man Who Went into the West,* p. 28 ff.

13 R.G. (1911) Census Return, Cardiff, RG78 PN1846 RD588 SD3 ED1 SN45.

14 R.G. (1891) Register of Births, 1891, Cardiff District, June Quarter, Vol. 11a, p. 696.

15 R.G. (1891) Census Return, Merthyr Tydfil RG12/4435/93.

16 R.G. (1898) Register of Marriages, 1898, Merthyr Tydfil District, Sept. Quarter, Vol. 11a, p. 735.

17 R.S. Thomas, 'No-One', p. 33.

18 R.G. (1901) Census Return, Merthyr Tydfil, RG13/50/166.

19 R.G. (1861) Census Return, Llanfabon, RG9/4046/65.

20 R.G. (1871) Census Return, Merthyr Tydfil, RG10/5393/10.

21 R.G. (1881) Census Return, Merthyr Tydfil, RG11/5311/60.

22 R.G. (1883) Register of Deaths, 1883, Pontypridd District, Dec. Quarter, Vol.11a, p. 229.

23 R.G. (1881) Census Return, Merthyr Tydfil, RG12/9435/51.

24 R.G. (1881) Register of Marriages, 1881, Merthyr Tydfil District, June Quarter, Vol.11a, p. 607.

25 R.G. (1861) Census Return, Llanwonno, RG9/4047/53.

26 R.G. (1871) Census Return, Llanwonno, RG10/378/5.

27 R.G. (1878) Register of Deaths, 1878, Merthyr Tydfil District, Sept. Quarter, Vol.11a, p .45.

28 R.G. (1876) Register of Marriages, 1876, Merthyr Tydfil District, Dec. Quarter, Vol. 11a, p. 567.

29 R.G. (1897) Register of Deaths, 1897, Merthyr Tydfil District, March Quarter, Vol. 11a, p. 386.

30 R.G. (1898) Register of Deaths, 1898, Merthyr Tydfil District, March Quarter, Vol. 11a, p. 401.

31 R.G. (1901) Census Return, Merthyr Tydfil, RG13/5027/746.

32 R.G. (1891) Census Return, Neath, RG12/12/4661/74; 1901, Census Return, Neath, RG13/5057/18.

33 R.G. (1891) Census Return, Merthyr Tydfil, RG12/4435/6; (1901) Census Return, Merthyr Tydfil, RG13/5027/44.

34 R.G. (1891) Register of Deaths, 1891, Merthyr Tydfil District, June Quarter, Vol. 11a, p. 436.

35 R.G. (1898), Register of Deaths, 1898, Merthyr Tydfil District, June Quarter, Vol. 11a, p. 309.

36 R.G. (1901) Census Return, Merthyr Tydfil, RG13/5027/44.

37 See R.S. Thomas, 'Former Paths' and 'No-one' in *Autobiographies* (London: Dent, 1997).

38 John Bowlby, *Attachment and Loss* (London: Pelican Books, 1957); *Childcare & the Growth of Love* (London: Penguin Books, 1961); Michael Rutter, *Maternal Deprivation Re-Assessed* (London: Penguin Books,1972); Michael & Marjorie Rutter, *Developing Minds: change & continuity across the lifespan* (London: Penguin Books, 1993); D.W. Winnicott, *The Child, the Family and the Outside World* (London: Penguin Books, 2000). See also, Barbara Prys-Williams, *Twentieth-Century Autobiography*, (Cardiff: University of Wales Press, 2004) pp. 126-127.

39 H.M. Courts Service *National Probate Calendar* 1861-1941, August 1898.

40 *Ibid*.

41 Gwydion Thomas, quoted in Byron Rogers, *The Man Who Went into the West,* p. 38.

42 R.S. Thomas, 'No One', p. 81 and Byron Rogers, *The Man Who Went into the West,* p. 74. Rogers gives no clear source for the claim that Margaret was educated in Wantage, which does not appear in R.S.'s 'Autobiographical Essay'. No other source for the claim has been found.

43 R.G. (1901) Census Returns, Wantage, RG13/1135/5;

1135/10; 1135/16; 1135/70.

44 R.G. (1901) Census Return, Merthyr Tydfil, RG13/501/166.

45 Crockford, *Crockford's Clerical Dictionary 1947* (London: Church House Publishing, 1947) p. 319.

46 R.G. (1892) Register of Marriages, 1892, Merthyr Tydfil District, Sept, Quarter, Vol, 11a, p. 813.

47 A codicil to Henry Roberts' will, dated 22 November, 1897, makes it clear that he had settled, unspecified, property on both Ann David and Ann Roberts, on 12 November, 1887, the same day as, but before he signed, his will. Neither codicil nor the will mentions the Maesyffynon house.

48 Gabriel Sewell, Deputy Librarian, Lambeth Palace Library, by email, September 2010; not until the Marriage (Enabling) Act of 1960 was it legal for a man to marry his deceased wife's aunt.

49 Llantwit Major church, Burial Register, 5 September, 1947, Louise Cordery, Archivist, of Glamorgan Archives, by email, 2 Sept., 2010.

50 R.S. Thomas, 'Salt', p. 395.

51 See note 49.

52 Crockford, *Crockford's Clerical Directory 1947,* p. 319.

53 R.G. (1891) Census Return, Merthyr Tydfil, RG12/43335/58.

54 R.G. (1881) Census Return, Upton-Upon-Severn, RG11/2922/107.

55 Crockford, *Crockford's Clerical Directory 1947,* **p. 319**.

56 R.S. Thomas, 'No One', p. 81.

57 It seems probable that Henry's promotion to the status of 'Gentleman' occurred either at the insistence of his daughter Ann, or on the initiative of an obsequious solicitor. Only a few years earlier, Henry had described himself to the census enumerator as a 'Retired Innkeeper', and his death certificate gives him as a 'Retired Licensed Victualler'.

58 H.M. Courts Service, National Probate Calendar, 1861-1941, September, 1898.

59 www.measuringworth.com (accessed 20 October, 2010).

60 R.S. Thomas, 'A Boy's Tale', *Collected Poems 1945-1990* p. 142.

61 R.S. Thomas, 'Former Paths', 'No One', *Autobiographies* (London, J.M. Dent, 1997) pp.7-8, 29; 'R.S. Thomas' Adele Sarkissian (ed.) Contemporary Author Autobiography,Vol.4 (Detroit, Gale Research Company, 1886) p. 301.

62 H.M. Courts Service, *National Probate Calendar* 1861-1941, Nov. 1887: Edmund Thomas left a net estate of £47,426 14s .0d., which, in 2010, would be worth between a minimum of £3,930,000 and a maximum of £52,000,000; www.measuringworth.com, (accessed 20 Oct. 2010).

63 R.S. Thomas, 'Former Paths', pp. 7-8.

64 Gwydion Thomas, quoted in Byron Rogers, *The Man Who Went into the West,* p. 38. The fact that these collectors are said to have called, 'with the regularity of Jehovah's Witnesses', suggests they may have been tallymen, (or insurance agents), rather than debt collectors.

'Playing the old anthropomorphic game':

R. S. Thomas's 'Middle Period' and the Rhetoric of Theological (Im)Possibility

Patrick Toal
Bangor University

> They spoke to him in Hebrew and he understood
> them; in Latin and Italian and
> he understood them. Speech palled
> on them and they turned to the silence
> of their equations. But God listened to them
> as to a spider spinning its web
> from its entrails, the mind swinging
> to and fro over an abysm
> of blankness.
>
> R. S. Thomas, from 'Dialectic', *Frequencies* (1978)

> 'What am I to do, what shall I do, what should I do, in my situation, how proceed? By aporia pure and simple? Or by affirmations and negations invalidated as uttered, or sooner or later?'
>
> Samuel Beckett, from *The Unnameable* (1959)

In the Winter 2008 edition of *Renascence*, the poet and critic Daven Michael Kari, in comparing the work of St. John of the Cross and R. S. Thomas, writes that 'both authors agree on the centrality of pain as a tool for heightening one's sensitivity to the spiritual world, and both seem to agree in their recognition of the extent to which God is unknowable to the rational mind'.[1] Leaving aside whether or not this relatively unadorned statement is actually true with regard to St. John of the Cross,[2] Kari's emphasis on the supposed 'unknowability' of Thomas's God – a contrast between, perhaps, Johannine 'knowledge' and Pauline 'faith'[3] – has been echoed by so many commentators that it has, in effect, attained the level of critical orthodoxy. In the popular consciousness (as many of the obituaries demonstrated) the poetry of Thomas is thematically reducible first of all to the Prytherch and 'Prytherch-like' verses from *The Stones of the Field* to Pietà and secondly to the Deus absconditus poems which increasingly embedded themselves within the poet's oeuvre from the penultimate Eglwys-fach volume (*The Bread of Truth*, 1963), through the Aberdaron period, and into his retirement on the Llyn Peninsula. As another critic has recently proposed, Thomas's apparent 'inability to conceive of God in human terms and the emphasis that his later poetry in particular places upon the extreme difficulty of coming into contact with the divine [...] is one of the most distinctive features of the poetry Thomas produced during the last thirty years of his life'.[4]

The nucleus of this argument primarily denotes, of course, Thomas's alleged religious ontology: the poet's God is absent, so the thesis runs, therefore any attempt to postulate meaningful statements concerning Him is either mere vanity (in the Ecclesiastian sense) or else a retreat, as it were, into the ineffability of mysticism.[5] One cannot 'think' God and in consequence one cannot 'say' Him; epistemic 'boundedness', lifting a phrase from Andre Kukla, necessarily entails ineffability and, because human beings very probably *are* epistemically bounded, there must also exist correspondingly ineffable states of affairs in human language, and it is to these that we are repeatedly directed by the poet.[6] Thomas's rhetoric of absence, appearing as it does to dovetail with contemporary scepticism concerning religious belief, has meaning in a way that kerygmatic affirmations of God's presence do not,[7] and his continual foregrounding of what Anne

Stevenson in her review of *The Echoes Return Slow* calls 'insistence on the dignity of his vocation, the equations he makes between religion and art, liturgy and poetry', are suggestive of a 'characteristic schism: Thomas the artist versus Thomas the man of God. Or perhaps better, Thomas the arrogant versus Thomas the humble. Or perhaps better still, art versus nature, but both bound into the incomprehensible nature of God.[8]

In what follows, I would like to suggest that much of Thomas's religious verse in his 'middle' or Eglwys-fach period (the religious poems from 1955-1966 not having received the same amount of detailed commentary as the Aberdaron and 'retirement' verses) is far from being as theologically, metaphysically or epistemologically 'negative' as a preliminary reading of the work would perhaps lead us to expect. In particular, I would like to argue that Thomas's portrayal of both the *via negativa* and its corollary, the *via positiva* – or, to implement slightly more specific terminology, apophatic (negative) and cataphatic (positive) religious discourse –form a linguistic-theological *symbiosis*. To elevate the former in our understanding of Thomas's work at the expense of the latter, is to significantly diminish what the poetry may impart to us concerning the essential dispositions of religious understanding and the numerous ways in which we comprehend, and simultaneously speak of, the nature of divinity. Thomas, I hope to show, is most decidedly not projecting a 'metaphysical' God – whether the God concerned be that of classical philosophical theism or a 'post-Nietzschean' *Deus absconditus* – but rather is interested in revealing the self-perplexing habits human cognition often employs to 'interpret' the divine and, through accentuation of an opposing dialectic, reveal how it *ought* to. In the poems of this period, the thematic keynote is often a 'deontologisation' of words,[9] which leads in turn to renewed focus upon our desire to erroneously anthropomorphize God – to play 'the old anthropomorphic game', as the Narrator says concerning our aspiration to sentimentalise nature in *The Minister*. This approach, if not checked, will lead us to further theological confusion and philosophic bewilderment. In the religious poems of this period Thomas, like his philosophical contemporary Wittgenstein in the *Philosophical Investigations* of 1953, is showing us 'a number of sketches of landscapes',[10] which, by encouraging us to travel through, should assist us in liberating ourselves from inauthentic theological understanding; to continue the Wittgensteinian gloss, Thomas is attempting to *clarify* the nature of our religious (pre)suppositions and, in so doing, 'show the fly the way out of the fly-bottle'.[11] Thomas is as such not renouncing theological knowledge, as his religious poems must be apprehended not merely as objects of interpretation but, at the same time, as *means* of interpretation, or, as Thomas himself put it, quoting approvingly Daniel Hoffman's reading of Edwin Muir, the purpose of the poet is to function as 'an *extractor* of meaning, not an imposer of willed unity upon experienced chaos'.[12]

To begin with a reference to the first of the Eglwys-fach volumes, *Song at the Year's Turning*, 'A Person from Porlock'[13] in the 'Later Poems' section, uses Coleridge's infamous encounter with his unwanted guest to submit the argument, well-known to many a student of post-structuralist literary theory, that all-encompassing clarity within language is never unreservedly possible. Identity here is fractured; the poet seeks 'contact with his lost self' but 'the mind's gloom' importunately forbids existential completeness, whilst the possibility of finding epistemological 'solidity' between signifier and signified is described as 'the long torture of delayed birth'. Thus, deciphering the poem as concerned not only with the nature of aesthetic inspiration but also as a portrayal of the limitations of language when faced with the transcendental, we may feel compelled to posit an argument within which, 'Language, man's habitual tool in this reaching towards God's identity, always falls short. God always eludes us, remaining a mystery in the silence at the heart of things ... no matter how much is achieved through imagination and meditation by the poet and mystic – there is always the gap, which is a kind of defence of God's integrity against his creatures'.[14]

The hypothesis of Thomas's God as a 'God of the gaps'[15] and therefore Thomas himself as 'doubting' Thomas or as purveyor, with grim and unwavering Thomist scrupulousness, of anti-theology against his will, as it were, is another critical speculation so ubiquitous that it has very seldom been challenged, although, of course, there are assorted variations upon the underlying theme.[16] Yet simply to regard Thomas's theological position to be one of intractable 'impasse' between the divine ontology of God on the one hand and human imaginative deficiency and accompanying linguistic fragility on the other, is to ignore significant swathes of his poetry which suggest that the human *mind* (as opposed to the emotions) may indeed appropriate the numinous, albeit in a 'non-predicative' manner; unlike Beckett's anonymous, metaphysically befuddled protagonist in *The Unnameable*, Thomas appears to be arguing that 'abortive' predication is a powerfully *successful* rhetorical and referential tool.[17] For example, the poem 'Coleridge', placed two poems before 'A Person from Porlock', uses as its thematic hinge the notion of Coleridge's 'vain philosophy' – presumably a reference to his 'Adamic' idea that words may embody rather than merely 'take the place of' things[18] – to suggest instead that nature ('the shrill voices from the sea') repels our attempts at taxonomy. Nevertheless, it would be mistaken to assume from this that Thomas is compounding the negative or 'apophatic' view of language presented in 'A Person from Porlock', for the two poems must clearly be viewed as forming an imaginative synthesis, within which attention is focused not so much on language's referential failure, as on the realization that what is actually at fault are the ways in which we *perceive* reality and therefore our *expectations* of language. It does not follow that merely because we cannot 'capture' the essence of a subject in a solitary word or phrase, the essence of whatever we are considering cannot be arrested in a different manner, a position made explicit in 'Autumn on the Land' which concludes:

> You must revise
> Your bland philosophy of nature, earth
> Has of itself no power to make men wise. (SYT, 106)

Here, understanding the natural world and, by extension, understanding the nature of selfhood and/or divinity, entails perceptual *revitalization*, a crucial theme in much of Thomas's poetry throughout his 'middle period' and clearly discernible in many poems within *Poetry for Supper*, the first Eglwys-fach collection proper.[19] The volume opens with 'Border Blues' and although the poem is not explicitly 'theological', the different 'voices' detectable therein – the poem itself, structurally as well as linguistically, being a 'volley of voices', as the speaker describes the somewhat sinister 'ladies from the council houses' in the poem's second section – presage what we could term the collection's general themes of shifting perspectival anchorage points, imagistic fluctuation and ontological multiplicity.[20] 'The Letter' (PS, 26), for example, is concerned with the impermanence of 'emphatic' definitions and the contrasting temperament of emotion and intellect ('And laying aside the pen, dipped/ Not in tears' volatile liquid/ But in black ink of the heart's well') whilst 'The View from the Window' uses the extended metaphor of painting to argue that we habitually refuse to see variation in nature, preferring instead to inflict an unambiguous, metaphysically unalterable interpretation on to our surroundings:

> All through history
> The great brush has not rested,

Nor the paint dried; yet what eye,
Looking coolly, or, as we now,
Through the tears' lenses, ever saw
This work and it was not finished? (PS, 27)

'The Journey' (PS, 30) continues this accentuation of the perceptually complex and therefore also metaphysically and epistemologically multifaceted, and is Thomas's first poem to treat overtly the supposed juxtaposition between 'faith' and 'reason'.[21] The poem has at its conceptual centre the long-established conceit of life as a process of travelling and therefore, it is hoped, arrival and discovery, but its connective tissue, both theologically and imagistically, is the further conceit that we are led astray from our final destination by a consuming desire to impose 'definitions' in order to make sense of religious consciousness and consciousness of religion:

And if you go up that way, you will meet with a man,
Leading a horse, whose eyes declare:
There is no God. Take no notice ...
                    the road runs on
With many turnings towards the tall
Tree to which the believer is nailed.

The 'many turnings' are what in the Prytherch poem 'Green Categories' (PS, 19) is additionally described as the Kantian 'War of antinomies', those contradictions in reasoning ascertained by Kant in his *Critique of Pure Reason* as a necessary consequence of any attempt to conceptualize the nature of transcendent reality.[22] However, it is important also to realise that contradiction is not cognate with meaninglessness, for contradiction discloses *fallacious* reasoning and therefore performs the important task of illuminating argumentative terms and the intellectual practices implanted within them. Far from being epistemically redundant, 'contradictory' thought processes direct us to *fresh* epistemic paradigms – and perhaps, ultimately, to a 'changing' of the '*episteme*', as Foucault calls it[23] – and thus should be used to *channel* thought rather than merely abrogate it. To prefer 'The easier rhythms of the heart/To the mind's scansion' ('Death of a Poet', PS, 31), is to elevate emotional commitment above intellectual comprehension and is, in a sense, an example of cognitive laziness for the religious thinker. Whether his theology be written in studious prose or the more capricious language of poetry, he has nevertheless a responsibility to explain the particular conception of God he entertains. It is hard to believe that Thomas is therefore simply advocating withdrawal into the type of epistemic 'silence' traditionally associated with the 'emotional' or 'mystical', as to do so would further imply that he regards onto-theological statements as non-cognitive and thus religious poetry itself as an epistemically vacuous language, a position which clearly does not coalesce with his many pronouncements, both in poetry and prose, to the contrary. In the 'religious' poems of *Poetry for Supper*, indeed, the emphasis is most emphatically not laid on the purely emotional. 'Absolution' (PS, 44), for example, reinforces the argument in 'The Journey' and 'Green Categories' that we are often so confused by emotion that we mistakenly privilege it over truth ('seeking what lay/Too close for the mind's lenses to see') while the final poem, 'Epitaph' (PS, 48), makes the unequivocal point that, 'The poem in the rock and/The poem in the mind/Are not one', thereby suggesting further the poet's fundamental role as 'synthesiser' of apparently discordant actualities.

In the 1961 volume *Tares*, 'Riposte' (*T*, 14), a poem structurally similar to 'Poetry for Supper' (*PS*, 34), rotates also on the twin themes of our predicative intelligence and the ways in which images are inherently imbued with the characteristic of constant renewal, each image within the poem being dependent on an opposite, or referential antonym, for its evocative power.[26] Here, the controlling metaphorical vehicle is again man's *perception* of nature, but the tenor fluctuates between the somatic ('there are things growing/Besides trees in this sweet world'), the psychological ('Look in the mind, green is showing'), and the verbal ('Employ nothing; your fault is speech'). Perspectives modulate and sharpen themselves upon the whetstone of predicative incongruity, so that when the opening image of the tree is returned to in the final stanza, it is appropriated with a rejuvenated awareness of how our descriptive modalities *themselves* are pivotal in the discernment of an object's metaphysical status, an idea also evident in the well-known second stanza of 'A Welsh Testament':

> Even God Had a Welsh name:
> We spoke to him in the old language;
> He was to have a peculiar care
> For the Welsh people. History showed us
> He was too big to be nailed to the wall
> Of a stone chapel, yet still we crammed him
> Between the boards of a black book. (T, 39)

This may be taken as an additional critique of Protestantism as 'the adroit castrator/of art', as Thomas disparagingly describes Luther's religion in *The Minister*, yet it is also possible – and arguably more important – to interpret the lines as illustrative of the poet's continuing concern with the possibilities of definition and, *a fortiori*, the nature of onto-theological classification or taxonomy. In 'Siesta' (T, 24), for example, the mind recoils at its obligation to discern an adequate language with which to conceptualize the divine, yet the pejorative tone of the concluding lines ('They saw it furnished with tall cloud,/And habitable by some huge presence/ At whose stature the mind balked') intimate that Thomas is not commending those who refuse to engage the challenge. A similar disputation is also apparent in 'Alpine' (T, 44), whose final, parabolic flourish, may be interpreted as a thematic coda for the volume in its entirety:

> A sense of smell is of less importance
>
> Than a sense of balance, walking on clouds
> Through holes in which you can see the earth
>
> Like a rich man through the eye of a needle.
> The mind has its own level to find.[27]

Emphasis on the mind – as opposed to the emotions – as the force which may unite or reconcile mutually incompatible definitions (or 'antinomies') is returned to in the third poem of *The Bread of Truth*, 'Welsh Border',[28] where Thomas again argues that 'The real fight goes on/ In the mind' and also in the twelfth, 'The Survivors', where the obvious usage in the first two stanzas of the Flood narrative with its affirmative implications of purgation and replenishment, is delicately undercut with the third and final stanza's depiction of the mariners' rescue:

> From the swell's rise one of them saw the ruins
> Of all that sea, where a lean horseman
> Rode towards them and with a rope
> Galloped them up on to the curt sand. (BT, 19)

Although the men have been liberated, the 'lean horseman' is redolent of the horsemen of the Apocalypse (the sense of religious tentativeness perhaps also galvanised by the epithet 'curt', suggesting brusqueness or, in a slightly different reading, that which is ephemeral) so that at the poem's conclusion sanguinity gives way to hesitation and salvific buoyancy is counteracted, if not by scepticism, then at least by some degree of theological misgiving. Again, the interpretative crux is located within our intellectual awareness of opposition or disjunction, the 'positive' collapsing into the 'negative' and vice versa to foreground through symbiosis the essentially bifocal nature of theological truth itself; hence, for the religious believer to posit *either* apophatic or cataphatic religious discourse as 'lexically' or metaphysically prior to its opposite, is to once again become enmeshed within a Gordian knot of self-cancellation. Thomas's dexterous manipulation of the Noah myth in 'The Survivors',[29] shows that as soon as we elevate *one* religious paradigm above all others (for example, 'God as absent'; 'prayer as waiting'; 'God as merciful/merciless') our theological understanding begins to collapse under the weight of internal inconsistency. With *rigidly* 'predicative' theology, God becomes, for example, either a purely abstract, intellectualised deity, with 'our worshipping/done in the cemetery/of a blackboard' as Thomas later describes 'formalised' theology in the ekphrastic poem 'The Oracle' in *Ingrowing Thoughts*,[30] or something similar to the young Joyce's anthropomorphised yet still withdrawn and unapproachable God, blithely unconcerned with humanity's welfare, refined out of existence and paring his fingernails. Both projections are of course theologically unsatisfactory, and in these 'middle period' poems Thomas appears to be approaching the problem of how we can meaningfully communicate God's attributes in a somewhat different and, one may argue, significantly original manner. Instead of projecting the immanent and metaphysically nonrepresentational God of classical theism – the 'I am', for example, of the Hebrew Tetragrammaton – Thomas is emphasising the different ways in which we choose to 'see' God and therefore, like the Biblical prophets, is ultimately interested in 'deconstructing' the idols; our emotional, philosophical and theological projections of God, if understood without acknowledgement of their mutually interpenetrative character, lead us to confusion (for example, 'God is all good but is content to let evil occur') or tautology (for example, 'God does what God does') for religious truth, like selfhood and divinity, should be approached through an understanding of its *relational* as opposed to merely foundational character.[31]

With this in mind, it is important to stress just how 'orthodox' – or, perhaps more accurately, 'non-heterodox' – Thomas's religious thinking in these 'middle period' poems appears to be. So many bottles of scholastic ink have run dry through descriptions of Thomas as 'archetypal agnostic' or as direct inheritor of Shavian 'religiousness without religion',[32] that it is easy to forget that throughout his career, Thomas was writing within and thus responding to, a *tradition* of 'negativity' or apophaticism which, in a specifically Christian matrix, can be traced at least to the fifth, or sixth, century *Mystical Theology* of pseudo-Dionysius, which is itself a dialectical counterbalance to his earlier *Divine Names*. In the latter text, pseudo-Dionysius states explicitly that, although 'we must not dare apply words or conceptions to this hidden transcendent God', we can, nevertheless, 'use whatever appropriate symbols we can for the things of God. With these analogies we are raised upward toward the truth of the mind's vision, a truth which is simple and one', which is then 'negated' in the Mystical Theology with the argument:

> ... we should praise the denials quite differently than we do the assertions. When we made assertions we began with the first things, moved down through intermediate terms until we reached the last things. But now as we climb from the last things up to the most primary we deny all things so that we may unhiddenly know that unknowing which itself is hidden from all those possessed of knowing amid all beings, so that we may see above being that darkness concealed from all the light among beings.

By means of these metaphors of concurrent ascension and descension, used throughout both texts as well as to some extent in *The Celestial Hierarchy*,[34] pseudo-Dionysius is arguing, as Denys Turner forcefully points out, that:

> the way of negation is not a sort of po-faced, mechanical process, as it were, of serial negation .... Rather ... the way of negation demands prolixity; it demands the maximisation, not the minimisation of talk about God; it demands that we talk about God in as many ways as possible, even in as many conflicting ways as possible, that we use up the whole stock-in-trade of imagery and discourse in our possession, so as thereby to discover ultimately the inadequacy of it all, deserts, silences, dark nights and all.[35]

In this sense, and as Turner in his article proceeds to stress, the apophasis of pseudo-Dionysius is dialectically contingent upon his own cataphatic theology and vice versa; the *via negativa* depends for its argumentative energy on its *own* negation and the *via positiva*, by a similar process of accentuation through referential redundancy, in turn projects us back to the *via negativa*, which will then dismantle itself to form a new antithesis-cum-thesis-cum-synthesis and so on, ad infinitum. Prolixity (in Turner's sense) demands rhetorical diversity and figurative variation, and in many of Thomas's 'middle period' poems also, the language employed often appears to indicate the essentially protean nature of both 'secular' and 'religious' consciousness themselves. In the crypto-nationalist poem 'Welcome' (BT, 24), a poem which may also be read as an extension of Thomas's ideas regarding the perceptual foundation of metaphysical taxonomy, the trope of truth as 'beyond' language is again brought into play – truth is 'the cold bud of water/ In the hard rock', the figure recalling the earlier 'The poem in the rock/And the poem in the mind' of 'Epitaph'[36] – but the verse doubles back upon itself between the first and second stanzas ('You can come in,/You can come a long way;/We can't stop you'...'There is no way there;/Past town and factory/You must travel back') and in so doing may be construed as demonstrative of rhetorical 'telescoping' or as emphasising the reciprocally *compatible* nature of imagistic 'conflation' *and* 'reduction'. Again, the stress is upon perspectival duality, leading, in turn, to an assertion that simplistic, monocular definitions not only mislead but energetically distort, a concern also evident in the irony-tinged, self-accusatory opening of 'Looking at Sheep':

> Yes, I know. They are like primroses;
> Their ears are the colour of the stems
> Of primroses; and their eyes –
> Two halves of a nut. (BT, 48)

Perception and therefore understanding is not a one-dimensional activity and in Pietà, the final Eglwys-fach volume, there are several poems which again exhibit at their conceptual axis the notion of 'singular' definitions as not only epistemically vacuous but metaphysically threadbare. 'Within Sound of the Sea' contrasts 'book-learning', that is, the lexicographer's formalized classifications of an object or entity, to non-denotative or non-predicative description, truth being located behind 'the print's bars' and 'reading' an activity self-consciously aware of itself as primarily performative:

> Am I wise now,
> With all this pain in the air,
> To keep my room, reading perhaps
> Of that Being whose will is our peace? (Pietà, 13)[37]

The theological amorphousness of the final line suggests that Thomas, like pseudo-Dionysius, is reluctant to ascribe 'settled' metaphysical features to his deity, but it does not follow from this that the deity referred to is either beyond meaningful description or is a mere willow-of-the-wisp of the imagination. What is under attack is not the truth of theism itself, but rather our craving to padlock theistic ascriptions within a solitary predicate, 'God is...', instead of cancelling the copula, so to speak, and recognise that truth lies between the polarities of apophatic and cataphatic discourse. In the collection's title poem, for instance (P, 14), the 'paradox' of Christ's broken body as simultaneously divine and human, with the personified Cross 'aching' for His return,[38] recalls the 'impossibility' of His two 'natures' – or the 'Hypostatic Union' – as articulated by the Chalcedonian Definition,[39] with the poet's visually swooping, peripatetic depictions ('hills', 'horizons', 'foreground') reinforcing the theme that in order to grasp the totality of an incident, scene or idea, one must view it from 'conflictive' perspectives.[40] The facing poem, 'Amen' (P, 15), further underscores this idea, the perspectival pluralism within each stanza tumbling synecdoche into metonymy, the abstract into the concrete and back again, to indicate that religious assent ('Accept; accept') lies within acknowledgment of the mind's largely 'polyvocalic', as opposed to 'monologic', construction and temperament. In the much-anthologised 'The Moor' (P, 24), Thomas further maintains that the mind's desire to stabilise itself through epistemologically 'undemanding' predication ('God is...') must be resisted, 'But stillness/of the heart's passions – that was praise/Enough; and the mind's cession/of its kingdom', with the poem's revelatory, verb-infused conclusion, 'the air crumbled/And broke on me generously as bread', indicative not of 'silent' introspection or compliant acceptance, but animatedly liberating religious praxis. Furthermore, to consolidate the general argument that selfhood and divinity are in effect dynamic, the trope of the natural world as liturgically effervescent – and therefore symbolically and perspectivally intricate – is picked up again and extended in the concluding stanza of 'Then' (P, 35), to suggest this time the sacramentally affirmative character of poetry's 'non-denotative' language:

> We wandered upon the broad hills'
> Back, crumbling the air's

Poetry. Nothing that nature
Did was a contradiction
That time, and the prey hung
Jewels of blood round the day's throat.

Several important poems from Thomas's 'middle period', then, metaphysically 'unstable' at their symbolic core, fundamentally paratactical and multi-layered, point not to the impossibility of meaningful religious discourse, but rather to how the 'impossibility' of God can be made *possible* through awareness of the self-rescinding, insufficient nature of *both* apophatic and cataphatic theological predication. Furthermore, *non*-predicative description of the syntactic form 'God is not...', is itself partly confirmatory, for, as Hugh Rayment-Pickard observes, 'discourses of negation are also affirmative, either echoing or *presupposing* the positivities they seek to deny by denials ... a purely negative discourse is not possible'.[41] With regard to this, our apophatic descriptions are themselves futilely anthropomorphic – despite our self-assurances to the contrary, we are back at 'playing the old anthropomorphic game' – for a statement of the form 'God is not...' is still an existential report and therefore vulnerable to referential collapse. Instead, Thomas appears to suggest in several of these 'middle period' poems, we must counterpoint each apophatic and cataphatic thought or proposition with its antonym – Thomas an inveterate 'counterpointer' of images and texts many years before *Counterpoint* appeared – because entrenched within any theological pattern of thought is a modality of perspectival displacement or transference, leading sequentially to a form of radical atropism (such as that detectable within 'Welcome' and 'Amen'), where tropes turn back into themselves to begin again their continual process of disruptive modulation, disjunction and differentiation. Thomas, therefore, similar in this sense to the scribes of Deutero-Isaiah with their iconoclastic arguments ('To whom can you compare God? What image can you contrive of him?' 40:18), is showing that 'impossibility' is a *meaningful* predicate and that the *via negativa*, if correctly apprehended, does not in any way lead to the metaphysical/existential denials of anti-theism or the epistemological 'silence' of the mystical. As St. Augustine himself wrote in a typically flighty excursion into anthropomorphism, religious truth 'is close to all its lovers throughout the world who turn towards it, and for all it is everlasting. It is in no place, yet nowhere is it absent'.[42]

NOTES

1 Daven M. Kari, 'R. S. Thomas and the Dark Night of the Soul: Song, Suffering, and Silence in a Life of Faith', *Renascence: Essays on Values in Literature*, 6: 60, No. 2 (2008), p. 105.

2 Gerald Brennan, for example, commenting on 'Llama de amor viva', argues that the poem shows that 'it is possible with time and practice to increase the degree of the love that nourishes that union [with God], just as when a fire, after taking hold of wood and transforming it by its heat into itself, still has the capacity to burn more fiercely'. *St. John of the Cross: His Life and Poetry* (London: Syndics of Cambridge U. P., 1973), p. 127.

3 Cf. John, 5: 13, 'I write this to you who believe (*pisteuousin*) in the name of the Son of God, that you may know (*eidete*) that you have eternal life'.

4 Sam Perry, ' "Hoping for the Reciprocal Touch": Intimations of the *Manus Dei* in the Poetry of R. S. Thomas', *Literature and Theology*, Vol. 21, No. 2, June (2007), p. 187. In much of the secondary literature the conceptual pivot of an absent God – or, a modification of this thesis, God as 'present within absence' – is employed repeatedly. See, for example, H. D. Lewis, 'The later poetry of R. S. Thomas', *Poetry Wales*, 14.4, (1979), pp. 26-30; Anthony Conran, *The Cost of Strangeness: Essays on the English Poets of Wales*

(Llandysul: Gomer Press, 1982), pp. 254-262, which also contrasts Thomas's ('middle period') work with the writings of St. John of the Cross; Roland Mathias, '*Via Negativa*: Philosophy and Religion in the Poetry of R. S. Thomas', in *Critical Writings on R. S. Thomas*, ed. Sandra Anstey (Bridgend: Seren, 1992), pp. 62-82; J. D. Vicary, 'Absence and Presence in the Recent Poetry of R. S. Thomas', in *Miraculous Simplicity: Essays on R. S. Thomas*, ed. William V. Davis (Fayetteville: University of Arkansas Press, 1993), pp. 89-101; M. Wynn Thomas, 'Irony in the Soul: The Religious Poetry of R. S [ocrates] Thomas', in *Agenda: A Tribute to R. S. Thomas*, 36, 2, (1998), pp. 49-69; Christine Meilicke, 'Dualism and Theodicy in R. S. Thomas' Poetry', in *Literature and Theology*, Vol. 12, No. 4, (1998), pp. 407-418; John Barnie, 'Was R. S. Thomas an Atheist Manqué?', in *Echoes to the Amen: Essays After R. S. Thomas*, ed. Damian Walford Davies (Cardiff: University of Cardiff Press, 2003), pp. 60-75.

5 Elaine Shepherd in *R. S. Thomas: Conceding an Absence. Images of God Explored* (Basingstoke: Macmillan, 1996), p. 136, makes the blunt statement that Thomas was indeed a 'mystic' and endeavours to circumvent interpretative difficulties associated with this reading by arguing that Thomas's unequivocal *denial* of 'mysticism' was mere 'modesty' on his part and that, in any event, 'his religious poetry has much in common with the characteristics of mysticism'. Part of the confusion surrounding this issue no doubt originates in Thomas's refusal to be, as he said in an interview with Simon Barker, 'cornered by these orthodoxarians who are out for blood' (Simon Barker, '*Probing the God-Space: The Religious Poetry of R. S. Thomas*', unpublished PhD thesis, University of Wales [Lampeter], Appendix II, p. 304). For example, responding to Lethbridge's prompt, 'You once said in an interview that you were a nature mystic' – a reference to the John Ormond interview, 'R. S. Thomas: Priest and Poet', in *Poetry Wales*, 7, No. 4 (1972), pp. 47-57 – Thomas replied: 'I mean, I'm

not a mystic. And here is grounds for misunderstanding and misinterpretation on the part of the critics and so on. I'm not a mystic and never claimed to be a mystic. I used the word (sic) "Nature Mystic" as some sort of attempt to describe what I get from nature'. 'R. S. Thomas talks to J. B. Lethbridge', in *Anglo-Welsh* Review, 74 (1983), p. 47.

6 Andre Kukla, *Ineffability and Philosophy* (Oxford: Routledge, 2005). On the important point regarding whether or not the ineffable is sayable, Kukla writes: 'When mystics claim to have an ineffable insight, they must be drawing a distinction between ineffability and conveyability, for no human insight can be unconveyable – the fact that the mystic entertains it is already proof that humans can be caused to entertain it', pp. 18-19. Cf. Steven T. Katz, *Mysticism and Philosophical Analysis* (London: Sheldon Press, 1978), p. 26: 'There are NO pure (i.e. unmediated) experiences. Neither mystical experience nor more ordinary forms of experience give any indication, or any grounds for believing that they are unmediated. That is to say, *all* experience is processed through, organized by, and makes itself available to us in extremely complex epistemological ways. The notion of unmediated experience seems, if not self-contradictory, at best empty'.

7 'Kerygmatic' meaning here the recitation of God's 'positive' or 'revelatory' actions, especially those associated with the manner in which God makes Himself known through the Incarnation.

8 *Poetry Wales*, 24.2 (1988), p. 67.

9 I am using 'ontology' in its Heideggerean sense meaning that which signifies 'Being'; therefore, linguistic 'deontologisation' refers to an awareness that words may not necessarily contain empirical or metaphysical denotation. For an interesting discussion on Heidegger's philosophy as a form of 'religious atheism' – a designation which many critics have also felt compelled to assign to Thomas – see Stephen Eric Bronner, *Of Critical Theory and its Theorists* (Oxford: Blackwell, 1994), chapter 6.

10 Ludwig Wittgenstein, *Philosophical Investigations*, trans. G. E. M. Anscombe (Oxford: Blackwell, 1968), p. ix.

11 Wittgenstein's startling metaphor for his aim in philosophy in paragraph 309 of the *Investigations*, ibid.

12 R. S. Thomas, review of Hoffman's *Barbarous Knowledge*, in *Critical Quarterly*, 9.12 (1967), p. 381. My emphasis.

13 *Song at the Year's Turning* (London: Hart-Davis, 1955), p. 103. Hereafter references are included in the text, abbreviated as SYT.

14 John Barnie, 'R. S. Thomas: *Later Poems, 1972-1982*', in *Poetry Wales*, Vol. 18, No. 4 (1985), p. 92. Barnie has taken his 'apophatic' critique of Thomas's religious verse to interpretative extremity, even to the point of imputing to him atheism. See his 'Was R. S. Thomas an Atheist Manqué?' although in the interests of balance it must be mentioned that in this later paper Barnie premises his 'negative' hypothesis not on linguistic/metaphysical arguments but primarily biological ones. Thomas's God, according to Barnie (and mirroring Hughes's God in *Crow*), is 'a robust, peevish and vengeful deity' for 'In a world where God is present only as an absence, it may be that he is absent in the more thoroughgoing sense of being nonexistent'. In addition, Christianity, Barnie continues, 'ironically fails to console, because the Christian religion has never been able to square itself with nature, and R. S. Thomas was too keen a thinker not to be aware of this', pp. 64-74.

15 The expression is Thomas's own, from 'Probings: An Interview with R. S. Thomas', Ned Thomas and John Barnie, *Planet*, 80 (April/ May, 1990), p. 45. Importantly, however, Thomas appends the following restriction to his own metaphor: 'this does not mean that each closure of a gap is a kind of erosion of the reality of God. There is the God of Ann Griffiths and Mother Theresa as well as of Augustine and Pascal.... I do contemplate or visualize or experience God as other than the last frontier waiting to be crossed', ibid.

16 See, for example, William V. Davis's excellent chapter, 'Gaps

in the Poetry of R. S. Thomas', in his *R. S. Thomas: Poetry and Theology* (Waco: Baylor U. P., 2007), pp. 85-98, and Rowan Williams's typically thought-provoking essay, '"Adult Geometry": Dangerous Thoughts in R. S. Thomas', in *The Page's Drift: R. S. Thomas at Eighty*, ed. M. Wynn Thomas (Bridgend: Seren, 1993), pp. 82-98.

17 'Non-predicative' and 'predicative' simply refer to the customary syntactical construction 'X is Y', where 'X' denotes the subject-term and 'Y' the predicate.

18 See, for example, Coleridge's letter to William Godwin, September 22, 1800: 'I wish you to *philosophize* Horn Tooke's system, and to solve the great Questions.... Is *thinking* impossible without arbitrary signs? & – how far is the word "arbitrary" a misnomer? Are not words &c parts & germinations of the Plant? And what is the law of their Growth? – In something of this order I would endeavour to destroy the old antithesis of Words & Things, elevating, as it were, words into Things, & living Things too'. Cited in William Keach, 'Romanticism and language', in *The Cambridge Companion to British Romanticism*, ed. Stuart Curran (Cambridge: Cambridge University Press, 1993), p. 110.

19 R. S. Thomas, *Poetry for Supper* (London: Rupert Hart-Davis, 1958). Hereafter references are included in the text, abbreviated as PS.

20 Tony Brown in *R. S. Thomas: Writers of Wales* (Cardiff: University of Wales Press, 2006), p. 60, has argued that 'Border Blues', 'utilizes the fragmented, multi-voiced technique of Eliot's *The Waste Land*. As in Eliot's poem, echoes from the past, from a time when cultural values were coherent and personal identity secure, resound in the consciousness of the protagonist, as he wanders alone through a world in which coherence and continuity have been replaced by fragmentation, spirituality by materialism and triviality'.

21 I am regarding 'The Question' in *The Stones of the Field* as more concerned with the distinction between faith and

'emotion', although a case could be made, of course, for arguing that in Thomas's distinctive onto-theology reason and emotion can never be completely separated. See, for example, D. Z. Phillips, *R. S. Thomas: Poet of the Hidden God* (London: Macmillan, 1986), pp. 123-124: 'If knowing God were a matter of intellectual assent, it ought to be possible to say, "I believe in God", without this having any effect whatever on one's life. But this would not correspond to anything akin to religious belief. The word "feeling" has been given such trite treatment in twentieth-century philosophy that mention of it is almost bound to mislead. Yet the poet is right in insisting that what needs to be made central are the affective contexts in which the need for God has its sense, and a man coming to God has its significance. Trying to argue for the existence of God by means of something like the argument from design seems fruitless. It does not bring one any nearer to God'.

22 One must tread cautiously here, however, for as Chris L. Firestone has demonstrated, contemporary Kantian studies often stress a movement 'away from the theologically pessimistic understanding of Kant on religion and theology...towards a more theologically affirming understanding'. 'Rational Religious Faith and Kant's *Transcendental Boundaries', in Transcending Boundaries in Philosophy and Theology: Reason, Meaning and Experience*, ed. Kevin Vanhoozer and Martin Warner (Hampshire: Ashgate, 2007), p. 78.

23 In his ground-breaking Inaugural Lecture at the College de France on December 2, 1970, Foucault said, 'the idea of the founding subject is a way of eliding the reality of discourse' and, further, that 'there is in our society, and, I imagine, in all others, but following a different outline and different rhythms, a profound logophobia, a sort of mute terror against these events, against this mass of things said, against the surging-up of all these statements, against all that could be violent, discontinuous, pugnacious, disorderly as well, and perilous about them – against this great incessant and

disordered buzzing of discourse'. 'The Order of Discourse', in *Untying the Text: A Post-Structuralist Reader*, ed. Robert Young (London: Routledge, 1990), pp. 65-66. One may certainly contend that Thomas is fully aware of this unremitting 'buzzing of discourse' and uses its sonorities as a structural and verbal leitmotif in many poems.

24 The word 'mystical' itself requires judicious consideration, as at the back of it lies the Greek root '*mu-*', meaning something closed, which with St. Paul became 'mysterion', a secret or mystery (*mystikos*), which in turn refers to the Gospel postulation of God's love for man as revealed through and within Christ, and therefore ultimately represents the possibility of man in communication or *dialogue* with God. Therefore, popular critical appellations such as 'Thomas as mystic' or 'Thomas as poet of absence' and so forth, require to be treated with a degree of hesitation that is perhaps not often observable.

25 See, for example, 'R. S. Thomas at Seventy', broadcast on BBC Radio 3, December 7, 1983, quoted in M. J. J. van Buuren, *Waiting: The Religious Poetry of Ronald Stuart Thomas, Welsh Priest-Poet* (Nijmegen: Katholieke Universitat van Nijmegen, 1993), pp. 178-180: 'If there is any contact with an eternal reality I don't want to limit that reality to personality. It is a bit like Wordsworth's Fourteenth book of *The Prelude* with his trip up Yr Wyddfa, Snowdon. It seemed to me a type of majestic intellect. This seems to be more what I am after...I think that every poet is haunted by this feeling of inspiration; that you can labour, as Yeats said in one of his poems, 'Adam's Curse', you can labour for hours and not produce the effect and then out of the blue, without you apparently doing very much about it, comes the good poem or the good lines'.

26 R. S. Thomas, *Tares* (London: Rupert Hart-Davis, 1961). Hereafter references are included in the text, abbreviated as *T*.

27 *Tares* contains several poems contrasting the 'mind' with the 'heart'; for example: 'Genealogy' (*T*, p. 16); 'The Face' (*T*, p.

17); The Musician' (*T*, p. 19); 'Those Others' (*T*, p. 31).

28 R. S. Thomas, *The Bread of Truth* (London: Rupert Hart-Davis, 1963), p. 9. Hereafter references are included in the text, abbreviated as *BT*.

29 The Noah myth later resurfaced in Thomas's work. Barry Sloan, for instance, comments that the penultimate line of 'Waiting' from *Frequencies* ('somewhere between faith and doubt') may be seen as 'a summary statement of the ambivalence...in so much of Thomas's work', with Thomas advocating a type of faith, 'that lies behind the metaphor of letting God's name go and waiting, just as Noah, a key Old Testament model of faith, let the dove go out across the flooded world and waited to see if it would return'. ('"The Discipline of Watching and Waiting": R. S. Thomas, Poetry and Prayer', in *Religion and Literature*, 34.2 (2002), pp. 31-42). This emphasis on 'silent hope' as the best that faith can offer, seems to disregard Thomas's explicitly 'positive' connection of the Noah myth to the confidence the writer *must* entertain if anything at all worthy of his efforts is to be achieved, as stated in 'Vocabulary', *Residues* (although I am assuming that when Sloan wrote his paper *Residues* had not yet been published): 'A new Noah, I despatch//you to alight awhile/on steel branches, then call/you home, looking for the metallic/gleam of a new poem in your bill'. (R. S. Thomas, *Residues*, ed. M. Wynn Thomas (Northumberland: Bloodaxe Books, 2002), p. 63). Alternatively, there is the poem beginning 'At the graves head' in *The Echoes Return Slow* (London: Macmillan, 1988) p. 43, which concludes: 'wings//of a dove daily/returning from its journey/over the dark waters/with green in its bill'.

30 R. S. Thomas, *Ingrowing Thoughts* (Bridgend: Poetry Wales Press, 1985), p. 30.

31 It is interesting to note that Paul Ricoeur's famous argument that we are inherently textually or narrative shaped, owes much, as Ricoeur himself said, to contemporary theology's emphasis on the rejection of, 'the dualistic and individualistic self of modernity, cut off from its rootedness

in the world. They [post-1945 scriptural theologians] see in this shift a recovery of a more Biblical, Hebraic sense of self as inherently embodied, interpersonal and social'. Cited in Dan R. Stiver, *Theology After Ricoeur: New Directions in Hermeneutical Theology* (Kentucky: Westminster John Knox Press, 2001), p. 185.

32 William V. Davis has used a paradigm of both Arnoldian and Shavian scepticism as an exegetical rallying point for his view that Thomas, 'again and again, presents us with one man, alone, lonely for and before God, calling across the gapped void between them, hoping beyond hope that, somehow, God will hear his "verbal hunger" and be moved – if not to respond, at least to listen,' *R. S. Thomas: Poetry and Theology*, p. 90.

33 *Pseudo-Dionysius, The Complete Works*, trans. Colm Luibheid (New Jersey: Paulist Press, 1987), p. 138.

34 For example: 'Since the way of negation appears to be more suitable to the realm of the divine and since positive affirmations are always unfitting to the hiddenness of the inexpressible, a manifestation through dissimilar shapes is more correctly to be applied to the invisible. So it is that scriptural writings, far from demeaning the ranks of heaven, actually pay them honour by describing them with dissimilar shapes so completely at variance with what they really are that we come to discover how those ranks, so far removed from us, transcend all materiality. Furthermore, I doubt that anyone would refuse to acknowledge that incongruities are more suitable for lifting our minds up into the domain of the spiritual than similarities are' ibid., p. 150.

35 'Apophaticism, idolatry and the claims of reason', in *Silence and the Word: Negative Theology and Incarnation*, ed. Oliver Davies and Denys Turner (Cambridge: Cambridge University Press, 2002), p. 17. My emphasis.

36 The lines are also reminiscent of ,'The poem shut,/Uneasy fossil,/In the mind's rock', in 'Poet's Address to the Businessmen', (*T*, p. 29).

37 R. S. Thomas, *Pietà* (London: Rupert Hart-Davis, 1966).

Hereafter references are included in the text, abbreviated as *P*.

38 It is worth mentioning that 'paradox' originally meant that which was contrary to expectations, thus 'marvellous' or 'incredible', and the Biblical *paradoxalogia* were tales of wonder, as in Luke 5: 26: 'amazement seized them all, and they glorified God and were filled with awe saying, "we have seen strange things (paradoxa) today."' See Hugh Rayment-Pickard, *Impossible God: Derrida's Theology* (Burlington, Vermont: Ashgate, 2003), 151. Cf. Rowan Williams, *Open to Judgement: Sermons and Addresses* (London: Darton, Longman and Todd, 1994), 119: 'We utter paradoxes not to mystify or avoid problems, but precisely to stop ourselves making things easy by pretending that some awkward or odd feature of our perception isn't really there. We speak in paradoxes because we have to speak in a way that keeps a question alive'. See also Williams's *The Wound of Knowledge* (Atlanta: John Knox Press, 1979), p. 2 – the title incidentally taken from Thomas's poem 'Roger Bacon' in *Frequencies* – where Williams argues that 'the goal of Christian life [is] not enlightenment but wholeness – an acceptance of this complicated and muddled bundle of experiences as a possible theatre for God's creative work'.

39 At the fifth session of the Council of Chalcedon in 451, it was decided as a matter of doctrinal truth that Christ simultaneously possesses two natures, the 'perfectly human' and the 'perfectly divine'.

40 It is surprising that little has been said in regard to Thomas's actual sequencing of poems within individual collections, as quite often one poem is dependent upon another for its allusive vigour. Taking as a brief sample poems from the Eglwys-fach period, 'The Slave' (SYT, p. 104) may be seen as companion piece to 'Autumn on the Land'; 'Temptation of a Poet' may be contrasted with 'Evans' (PS, pp. 14, 15); 'Chapel Deacon' with 'The Country Clergy' (PS, pp. 17, 28); 'Composition' with 'The Cure' (PS, pp. 40, 41); 'The Conductor' with 'The Musician' (T, pp. 13, 19); 'Country

Cures' with 'Funeral' (BT, pp. 8, 10); 'Becoming' with 'Parent' (BT, pp. 14, 28); 'A Country' with 'Movement' (BT, 30, 35); 'For Instance' with 'Ravens' (P, pp. 21, 22); 'The Visit' with 'Exchange' (P, pp. 30, 31). It is arguable that this criss-crossing of themes and conceits and 'counterbalancing' of one poem by another, shows Thomas's desire to provide more than one metaphorical appropriation of a subject, thereby strengthening his general idea that simplistic categorisations and descriptions must be repudiated in favour of the metaphysically and linguistically multifaceted.

41 *Impossible God*, p. 127. My emphasis.

42 St. Augustine, *De gratia et libero arbitrio* II. 13. 35. Cited in Aidan Nichols, *A Grammar of Consent: The Existence of God in Christian Tradition* (London: University of Notre Dame Press, 1991), p. 61.

Harri Webb and the Poetry of Lorca

Gwynne Edwards
Emeritus Professor, University of Aberystwyth

Having written previously about Vernon Watkins's interest in the poetry of the great Spanish poet Federico García Lorca and his translation of two of Lorca's poems, I discovered not long afterwards that Harri Webb, the Swansea-born poet, had translated no fewer than ten.[1] These belong to the period between 1947, when Webb was twenty-seven years old, and 1954. Although he lived for another forty years, he translated no more Lorca poems, though translations or adaptations of poems by French, Breton, Provençal, Sardinian, Galician, and Catalán poets continued to appear until 1975. What, then, was the source of Webb's early interest in Lorca's poetry; why did he translate the work of many other European poets; and what is the quality of his translations of Lorca?

At the age of eleven, Webb became a pupil at Glanmor Secondary Boys' School, Swansea, where he proved to be less than competent in Arithmetic, Algebra and Geometry, took no interest in sport, but was a high-flyer in English, French and Spanish. From Glanmor School, he proceeded to Magdalen College, Oxford, where he read Medieval and Modern Languages, specializing in French, Spanish and Portuguese. Later on, he would describe both his schooldays and his time at Oxford:

> [At Glanmor] French was taught superbly, with a good accent and in a lively manner, stimulating an interest that filled my life for many years and is still among my chiefest pleasures...We learnt Spanish too, another window flung open on an unsuspecting world, one I could not enter as fully as the other, but providing, as it happened at that time, a more vivid stimulus: Lorca. Not that he was on the

> syllabus, of course. But the *Romancero gitano* [*Gypsy Ballads*] came into my hands, in a poorly produced commemorative volume brought out soon after his murder. Here now was a poet of my own day, a poet of his own people, killed, as far as I could make out, simply because he was such a poet. His death seemed part of the poetry itself. It meant more to me than anything I had encountered so far in the three literatures with which I was beginning to become acquainted. Later, at Oxford, I talked about him with don Alberto Jiménez. His teacher and mine, a circumstance which I still find incredible.[2]

The 'vivid stimulus' which Webb received from his acquaintance with Lorca's *Romancero gitano* can be explained in several ways. Of this volume Robert Havard has observed that 'its exceptional popularity owes much to its colourful evocation of Andalusia, Lorca's native province and Spain's gypsy heartland famed for flamenco dancers, bullfighters and tall Moorish towers'.[3] In addition, the poems, both in the *Romancero gitano* and in other collections, were, as Webb observed, of the people in the sense that they drew on traditional sources and could be recited aloud in the manner of a long-established tradition of oral poetry, as can so many of Webb's own poems. The *Romancero gitano* also contained characters and described events which were not only vividly drawn but which also, as in the case of the Andalusian gypsy and his way of life, appealed to the common man much more than to the sophisticated bourgeois. And again, Lorca's death in 1936 at the hands of Franco's fascist sympathisers in the early months of the Spanish Civil War combined with the allusions to fate and death which permeate the collection to invest him with the aura of self-prophesying victim, thereby adding to the appeal of both the man and his work.

This said, Webb's interest in Lorca, and in particular his subsequent translations of some of his poems, can also be explained in another way. If the initial attraction was in part that of someone with a rather Romantic sensibility, this later became something rather different. Webb's first translations were completed some ten years after his schoolboy discovery of the Spanish poet and continued for another seven years. In 1946, at the age of twenty-six, Webb had been demobilized from the navy and found himself in Scotland, with no idea of what he was going to or wanted to do, as Brian Morris has noted: 'The world lay all before him, but he had no place to go, and the next twelve months may well have been one of the most depressed and impotent periods of his life'.[4]

On the other hand, it was in Scotland that he discovered the poetry of the nationalist and communist Scottish poet, Hugh MacDiarmid, which fired in Webb a new enthusiasm for life and an intense interest in political attitudes towards his own country, Wales. In 1948 he joined Plaid Cymru, moved to the Welsh Republican movement in 1949, and in 1953 became a member of the Labour Party. The years in which he produced his translations of Lorca were, then, years in which he became intensely nationalistic, progressively anti-English, and much more open to European movements and ideas in both politics and literature. Looking back to his initial contact with the latter, he subsequently wrote as follows:

> I was studying the literatures of France and Spain, the product of markedly different cultures, different historical circumstances. This helped me to understand that the literature of England, for all its accessibility, was equally the product of a people completely differently circumstanced from our own [the Welsh] and, overwhelmingly, of one class of that people. Its working-class authors, such of them as there were, all went mad or committed suicide.[5]

Harri Webb's original poetry was for the most part of two kinds. He was, on the one hand, a poet steeped in the 'bardd gwlad' tradition, a term which Brian Morris has described as 'sometimes applied to a poet without much formal education, whose poems praise his particular locality, and the events, the births, marriages, deaths, scandals, achievements which took place there'.[6] Although extremely well educated, Webb wrote many poems in this tradition, of which 'Not to be used for babies', a poem about a local milkman, is a good example. The poem begins like this:

> Old Glyn, our milkman, came down from the country
> Between Waunarlwydd and Mynydd Bach y Glo
> A neighbour of innumerable uncles and cousins
> In an untidy region of marsh and pasture and mines...[7]

But then, in a manner very characteristic of Webb, the poem's local setting takes on a broader meaning and gradually becomes a more wide-ranging reflection on the golden days of boyhood:

> ...The spokes of his light trap
> And the big brass churn amidships shone in the sun
> And his brisk mare Shân was a champion trotter;
> And when I took the reins of a Saturday morning
> ....
> I drove the chariot of the sun, I was Caesar, Ben Hur...[8]

Of the 'bardd gwlad' tradition, Brian Morris has noted that 'the local in no way precludes the universal'.[9] And the same is true, of course, of the 'serious poems' which, to the consternation of many critics, appeared side by side with the 'bardd gwlad' pieces in the various collections of Webb's poetry. Don Dale-Jones has observed in this respect that 'An interest in Europe is common among Anglo-Welsh writers of the Harri Webb/Harri Jones generation ... and a natural characteristic of Welsh nationalism'.[10] But while Webb's 'serious' poems often have a European connection, they also frequently possess a resonance which goes beyond Europe.

The point is well illustrated in three poems written as far apart in time as 1944 and 1989. In 'At Aden', written in 1944, Glamorgan is held to be more beautiful than South Yemen:

> Though glare and sweat here blind my eyes
> Yet they a precious vision hold:
> Cool green Glamorgan far outlives
> The dazzlement of Sheba's gold. (*CP* 8)

In 'Anial Dir', written in 1949, the hills of the Rhondda Valley are reminiscent of the land of Canaan:

> The last of evening gently fills
> The silence when the changing hills
> One black one green on either hand
> Like Ebal and Gerizin stand. (*CP* 21-3)

In 'Four Castles', written in 1972, the castles of Caernarvon, Caerphilly, Harlech, and Cardiff are seen in the context of history, in particular in relation to the Roman occupation of Wales and the struggle against the English. And in Webb's very last poem, 'Dowlais', his discovery of the place where he was to live for forty years is described as just as dazzling and significant as the expeditions of Vasco da Gama:

> That lift of wonder in the Lusiads
> When all the marvels of the eastern sea
> Sparkled and shone in endless mystery
> To daze the hungry eyes of Vasco's lads
> ....
> Was mine when on an iron January day
> I first saw Dowlais on its iron hill
> And all was iron, like its history... (*CP* 375)

Similar connections between Wales and other countries are also to the forefront in Webb's translations of European poets. In 'Sonnet', a translation dated 1946 of a French poem by José-María Heredia, there may be no specific mention of Wales, but some of the lines are a clear pointer to the stagnation of the Welsh people, echoing Webb's political concerns and his frequently stated belief that, simply to survive under English domination, they had adopted 'a way tainted with servility, evasiveness, mysticism and a lack of moral fibre':[10]

> But man, forgetful of his forebears' fears,
> Will hear unmoved the sea the calm night long. (*CP* 11-12)

Similarly, there is no allusion to Wales in Webb's translation of Manuel María's 'Galicia', dated 1974, but the references to the people as the guardians of nationhood and identity could not be clearer:

> We who are the people
> Will be so eternally.
> In the people is the truth.
> Only to the people is it given
> To guard the essential
> Indestructible Galicia. (*CP* 233-4)

And the same identification with Wales runs through the translation, completed a year later, of 'A Peal of Bells', by the Catalán poet, Joan Colomines:

> But away with sadness, it is tomorrow that calls,
> And a song fills the air with a flight of voices,
> A peal of bells, the swirl of the dances
> To the sound of bagpipes, the dance of life.
> For tomorrow is coming, wreathed with sea-blue,
> Catalunya eternal, Catalunya and ourselves.
> Away with sorrow,
> Freedom beckons us to the destined centuries. (*CP* 248-9)

In general, Webb's translations of European poems cover three decades, from 1946 to 1975, and are of different kinds, but many of them link the thoughts and feelings of a Welsh poet to the European classical past, to contemporary European literary and cultural movements, and to European nationalism in its various forms. What Webb does not do, significantly, is connect his work to the English poetic tradition.

In seeking to establish such links, Webb was not alone among Welsh poets, as M. Wynn Thomas has noted: 'Webb's Wales ... like that of [Saunders] Lewis, was very much situated on an international map'.[11] In a similar manner, although he was temperamentally and ideologically very different from Webb, Vernon Watkins also found inspiration in European poetry. Having entered the University of Oxford at the age of eighteen, he, like Webb, studied Modern Languages – French and German specifically, though Gwen Watkins has indicated to me that he also acquired a knowledge of Spanish.[12] Leaving Oxford after only one year, Watkins suffered a severe nervous breakdown and, having recovered, sought to overcome the temporal chaos in his life by striving to see the problems of everyday existence as merely part of a universal pattern. Ian Hilton has noted as follows: 'His own poetry seeks to overcome the limitations of time and place in an attempt to achieve a visionary contemplation of life and death'.[13] In this respect, Watkins connected closely with the European symbolist movement in poetry and in the course of his writing produced almost two hundred translations of European poems, including translations of poems by Hölderlin, Heine, Rilke, Baudelaire, Rimbaud and Valéry. In his original poetry too, Welsh backgrounds and places were invested with symbolic and archetypal significance, as in the following lines from 'Ballad of the Equinox':

> Pwlldu – an eternal place!
> The black stream under the stones
> Carries the bones of the dead...[14]

In the sense that their involvement in the translation of European poetry both strengthened their convictions and enriched their own work, Watkins and Webb, despite their differences, were kindred spirits.

Watkins translated only two of Lorca's poems, 'Ballad of the Little Square' and 'Song of the Dark Doves', though he admired many others. In the first of the two poems, he clearly identified with a theme which runs through Lorca's work in general: the loss of childhood innocence and the difficult transition to adulthood, with all its problems of frustration, pain, and ultimate death. In the second poem he responded to Lorca's evocation of the enigmatic nature of human existence, something with which Watkins was all too familiar. Lorca's poetry, then, provided the Welsh poet both with a biographical connection and a poetic voice which transformed the personal and the particular into a statement which linked all men in time and space.[15]

Of Harri Webb's attraction to the poetry of Lorca, Meic Stephens has written as follows:

> García Lorca (1898-1936), the great Spanish poet and playwright, was one of Harri Webb's favourite writers, perhaps because his poetry achieved immense popularity through recitation ... these poems are based on folk-motifs and folk-songs from Andalusia, and their enigmatic quality is part of their charm.[16]

This observation is mostly true of the seven poems which Webb translated from Lorca's collection of ninety poems, *Canciones* (Songs), published in 1927, though, as we shall see, the poems are characterised by rather more than charm. Webb grouped five of the seven poems under the title 'Five Songs', while the other two are free-standing.

The other three of Webb's ten translations come from Lorca's collection of eighteen poems, *Romancero gitano*, published in 1928, and which Webb had so much admired at school. In nine of the ten poems, the theme of childhood is much to the fore, the one exception being 'Tamar and Amnon', which is based on the Biblical story of Amnon's attraction to and rape of his half-sister.

The first three of Webb's 'Five Songs' belong to a section of Lorca's *Canciones* entitled 'Nocturnos de la ventana' ('Night at the Window'). The suggestion of peace and tranquillity evoked by the Spanish title, and associated in particular with piano music, is progressively challenged in the course of the three poems. The first of them captures the voice of the innocent and imaginative child who looks out through the bedroom window in a simple, straightforward way and swiftly transfers his or her attention from one object to another:

> Moon go high,
> Wind go low:
> Exploring sky
> My long looks go. (*CP* 14)

In the second poem the world outside the window is seen to enter the child's bedroom in a much more ominous way, and there is also a suggestion, in the phrase 'clock-wounded moments', of the intrusion of a more adult voice looking back:

> An arm of the night
> Comes in through the window
> A long dark arm
> With pulses of water.
> On blue crystal river
> My soul played,
> Clock-wounded moments
> Fade. (CP 14)

The third poem points to a further stage in childhood in which the child, far from remaining passive in relation to whatever dangerous forces may exist beyond the window, takes the risk of challenging them:

> I put my head
> Out of the window and see
> The wind's knife wish
> To behead me.
> In the invisible
> Guillotine
> I put the blind
> Heads of my wishes. (*CP* 14)

The other two poems which Webb included in 'Five Songs' come from two different sections of Lorca's *Canciones*. In the first of these, entitled 'Mad Song', a child wishes to become water, then silver, and is warned by its mother of the dangers inherent in such desires. In the second poem, for which Webb changed Lorca's more suggestive 'Cortaron tres árboles' ('They Cut Down Three Trees') to 'Air', three trees are cut down one after the other:

> Three
> (axes of day)
> two
> (silver wings play)
> one
> none
> (bare waters stay). (CP 15)

This poem was translated by Webb in 1947 and belongs, therefore, to the period when he was, as Brian Morris has stated, in a state of 'indecision and depression'.[17] In Lorca's work in general, trees which are cut down – consider the significance of the Woodcutters in *Blood Wedding* – symbolize the way in which human beings succumb to the intervention of fate, and, for all its playful surface, 'Cortaron tres árboles' is an early example of that theme. In choosing to translate this poem, Webb seems to have identified with Lorca's pessimism.

The two remaining poems which complete the seven which Webb selected from Canciones, 'Fable' ('Fábula') and 'Horseman's Song' ('Canción de jinete'), are also very much to do with childhood. 'Fable' expresses childhood fears and the nightmarish world of dreams, while 'Horseman's Song' is a tale told or sung to a child of a rider who, on his way to Córdoba, becomes increasingly aware of the inevitable death that awaits him – a tale, in short, told to a child but infused with adult fears:

> Córdova.
> Far and lonely.
>
> Black horse, full moon,
> olives in my saddlebag.
> Although I know the roads
> I shall never reach Córdova.
>
> On the plain, in the wind,
> black horse, red moon.
> Death is watching me
> from the towers of Córdova.
>
> Ah, the road is long!
> Ah, my horse is brave!
> Ah, Death is waiting for me
> before I reach Córdova!
>
> Córdova.
> Far and lonely. (*CP* 32)

Quite clearly, Lorca's poems are more than mere echoes of folk-songs popular in Andalusia. They often evoke the fearful world of the child's imagination, be that child awake or asleep, and at times they suggest the voice of the adult who projects his or her fears into the stories and songs directed to the child. G.G. Brown has made the following observation in relation to *Canciones*:

> [They] reveal that Lorca's interest in the folklore of childhood, and in the kind of response children make to verse and song, is an adult and sophisticated one ... It is far from his purpose to reproduce naïve songs of innocence. Themes of frustration, loss and death throw dark shadows over the playfulness of the poems.[18]

Two of the three poems which Webb translated from Lorca's *Romancero gitano* again evoke the darker side of childhood. 'Ballad of the Moon' ('Romance de la luna, luna') has as its subject the abduction of a child by the moon, which comes down to the gypsy forge, entrances the child with its voluptuous dance, and then leads him away through the sky. The poem is based, in part, on the popular superstition that the moon steals children who gaze at it too much, but Lorca also regarded the moon as a powerful influence on human destiny which ultimately brings death, and, in that respect, as a powerful force of Nature. In this context, 'Ballad of the Moon' can be seen to be a more developed and complex form of some of the short poems in 'Nocturnos de la ventana' and also as expressing a child's fearful dream of approaching danger.

'Preciosa and the Wind' ('Preciosa y el aire') also portrays a menacing natural force, in this case the wind, which pursues and attempts to seduce a young and innocent gypsy girl:

> Girl let me lift
> your dress to see you
> let my old fingers
> open the blue

rose of your belly.
Preciosa throws
her music away
runs without stopping
the huge wind after her
with a hot sword. (*CP* 18-19)

The girl succeeds in escaping her pursuer by taking refuge in the house of the English consul, a much more polite and reserved gentleman, while outside the lustful and frustrated wind vents its rage on the roof tiles. Once more the story owes something to popular culture, as well as to classical sources – the wind is a Dionysian satyr or Silenus – but Lorca clearly used it too to suggest the sexual fears of a young girl as she moves towards adulthood. Again, the poem has all the characteristics of a frightening dream.

Given this emphasis on childhood in nine of the ten poems chosen by Webb for translation, it seems unlikely that the choice was accidental. Only the tenth poem, 'Tamar and Amnon', falls outside the pattern, but since this poem focuses on Amnon's irresistible attraction to Tamar, it could be argued that this is the kind of adult experience of sexual desire to which a young girl like Preciosa will be exposed and which she has already seen embodied in the lustful wind. But if this is a possible interpretation, the poem also possesses another dimension. In the early 1920s, Lorca was immersed in the writings of Freud, and therefore in the workings of the unconscious mind and its expression in dreams,[19] which meant in turn that his poems, despite their traditional sources, were also firmly placed in a significant European intellectual tradition. Furthermore, the Freudian influence, precisely because the childhood fears and anxieties which he described are common to children everywhere, transformed the Spanishness of Lorca's poems into something much more archetypal and universal. This broader resonance, combined with their dramatic, colourful and exotic qualities, could well have attracted Webb to these poems, thereby enabling him to bond with a particular strand of European and, above all, non-English poetry.

As far as the art of translation is concerned, it is instructive to consider Webb's translations of Lorca in relation to others available at the time. Webb, as a student of Spanish at Oxford between 1938 and 1941, could well have seen the translations published in 1937 by A.L. Lloyd: *Federico García Lorca*, *Lament For the Death of a Bullfighter and Other Poems*, the other poems consisting of five from *Romancero gitano*, including 'Preciosa and the Wind'.[20] Two years later, *Poems by F. García Lorca, with English Translation by Stephen Spender and J.L. Gili* was also published in London, the collection consisting of thirty-one poems and seven poetic passages from Lorca's plays, but containing only one of the poems translated by Webb: 'Tamar and Amnon'.[21] But if, as seems likely, Webb was aware of these translations – as Vernon Watkins certainly was – his command of Spanish meant that he had no need to depend on them when he came to translate the poems of his choice, a likelihood confirmed by the fact that of the ten poems he chose to translate, only two appeared in the published volumes.

Unlike Vernon Watkins, Webb neither spoke nor wrote about the problems of translating Spanish verse into English. One particular problem, for example, concerns the frequency in Spanish verse of assonance, whereby in a poem's alternate lines the final word has its penultimate vowel stressed and its final vowel unstressed, a pattern which is maintained by Lorca throughout 'Preciosa and the Wind'. The first four lines of his poem illustrate the point:

> Su luna de pergamino
> Preciosa tocando vi<u>e</u>ne,
> Por un anfibio sendero
> de cristales y laur<u>e</u>les.[22]

Although Webb made no observation on the difficulty of preserving assonance when translating Spanish poems into English, his translations suggest that he was well aware of the problem. At all events, it is useful to compare his translations of 'Preciosa and the Wind' and 'Tamar and Amnon' with those by Lloyd and Spender and Gili in order to assess their merit.

In the early part of the first of the two poems, Lloyd translates Lorca's description of the carabineers and the gypsies who live in the high peaks thus:

> Upon the peaks of the mountains,
> the carabineers are asleep,
> guarding the white towers
> where the English people live.
> And the water gypsies
> have built, to pass the time,
> arbours of snail shell
> and branches of green pine. (*Lament* 29)

In comparison, Webb omits two phrases: 'are asleep' and 'to pass the time':

> High on the sierra
> the carabiniers
> guard the white towers
> where the English live
> the gypsies by the water
> are building
> grottoes of shells
> and green pine branches. (*CP*18)

In the latter part of the poem, when Preciosa escapes the wind by running into the English consul's house, Lloyd's translation contains two errors: 'fallen stars' and 'their caps in their hands':

> See where he comes,
> the satyr of the fallen stars,
> with his shining tongues!
>
> Preciosa, full of fear,
> runs into the house in which,
> far above the pines,
> lives the Consul of the English.
>
> Startled by her cries,
> Three carabineers come.
> Their black coats are belted
> and their caps in their hands. (*Lament* 31)

Webb corrects both errors:

> see he is coming
> satyr of the nearer stars
> with shining tongues.
>
> Preciosa fearful runs
> to the house
> of the English consul
> that stands high in the pines.
>
> Carabiniers come
> alarmed at her cries
> their black cloaks caught up
> their caps over their eyes. (*CP* 19)

In the poem's final lines, Lloyd's 'And while to those around her/weeping she tells her tale'(31) is translated by Webb as 'And while she is telling/her story crying/to that strange gentleman'(19). Although Lorca's 'aquella gente' could refer to a number of people, literally 'those people', it could also, in popular usage, refer somewhat sarcastically to a single person and suggests Webb's excellent knowledge of Spanish.

Webb's translation of Lorca's poem is, then, despite the omission of a few phrases, more accurate than Lloyd's, and it is also more concise: 'High on the sierra' instead of 'Upon the peaks of the mountains'; 'Girl, let me lift/your dress to see you'(18) instead of 'My child, that I may see you,/let me lift up your clothes'(29); and 'The Englishman gives/her a glass of milk/and a glass of gin'(19) rather than 'The Englishman gives to the gypsy/a pitcher of warm milk/and a glass of gin also'(31). In general, Webb's version is simpler, more concise, less ostentatiously literary than Lloyd's, and closer to Lorca's original. It drives the narrative forward, and in its unforced simplicity captures more effectively the popular spirit of Lorca's poem, as the opening of Webb's translation suggests:

Lloyd	Webb
Beating upon her tambourine Preciosa strolls Along an amphibious path Of crystal and laurels. Shattered by her playing the starless silences fall in the beating singing sea with its night full of fishes. (*Lament 29*)	Preciosa playing a moon of parchment walks the half watery pathway of crystals and laurels. The silence is starless and fleeing her tambourine it falls where the sea is beating and singing its night of fishes. (CP 18)

As far as versification is concerned, neither Lloyd nor Webb employ Lorca's octosyllabic line, the traditional line length of the Spanish ballad. Nor do they attempt Spanish assonance, though in Lloyd's version there are some sporadic examples of a kind of assonance which may be coincidental – 'pale', 'shade', 'milk', 'drink', 'tale', 'slate' – as well as of occasional rhyme – 'time', 'pine', 'clothes', 'rose'. Webb similarly has a few examples of both: 'fleeing', 'sea', 'stopping', 'sword'; 'you', 'blue', 'cries', 'eyes', but again they do not form a consistent pattern.

Spender and Gili's translation, 'Thamar and Amnon', begins as follows:

> The moon turns in the sky
> over lands without water
> while the Summer sows
> murmurs of tiger and llama.
> Above the roofs
> nerves of metal were sounding.
> Corrugated air came
> with the bleating of wool.
> Earth offers itself full
> of cicatrized wounds,
> or shaken by acute
> cauteries of white lights. (*Poems* 51)

Webb's translation reads thus:

> The moon moves over
> lands without water
> while summer murmurs
> of tiger and flame.
> Above the roofs
> rang nerves of metal.
> The air drifts
> with the bleating of sheep.
> The earth is full of wound scars
> shuddering with the intensity
> of white lights. (*CP* 34)

For the most part, the Spender/Gili translation is accurate enough. 'The moon turns in the sky', 'Corrugated air', 'the bleating of wool', 'cicatrized wounds', 'acute/cauteries of white lights' are all examples of more or less literal translations of Lorca's original phrases. Webb, as in 'Preciosa and the Wind', tends to simplify, omitting what he regarded as awkward and stilted words and phrases when translated into English – 'Corrugated', 'cicatrized', 'cauteries'. Indeed, even if the Spender/Gili version is closer to Lorca, it is not always as effective as Webb's. The latter's 'Above the roofs/rang nerves of metal' is in its hard sound and concision much more evocative than the rather limp and literal 'Above the roofs/nerves of metal were sounding', as is the languid effect of 'The air drifts/with the bleating of sheep' in comparison with 'Corrugated air came/with the bleating of wool'. In short, Webb's version reads like a poem in its own right while the Spender/Gili translation reads like a translation. Furthermore, the latter contains a really bad error which Webb translates accurately. In the lines 'while the Summer sows/murmurs of tiger and llama', Spender and Gili fail to realise that 'llama' is the Spanish word for 'flame' and seem to believe that a South-American animal has been magically transported to the Middle East.

Later in the poem, the Spender/Gili translation of the opening dialogue between Amnon and Tamar is again generally accurate:

> 'Thamar, efface these eyes
> with your fixed dawn.
> My threads of blood weave
> frills over your lap'.
> 'Leave me in peace, brother.
> Your kisses in my shoulder
> are wasps and light breezes
> in a double swarm of flutes'.
> 'Thamar, in your high breasts
> two fishes are calling me,
> and in the tips of your fingers
> there are murmurs of sealed rose'. (*Poems* 54-5)

Webb's version is:

> 'Tamar, stop my eyes
> with your immoveable dawn.
> My blood is weaving
> flounces on your gown'.
> 'Leave me be, brother.
> On my shoulder your kisses
> are wasps and breezes
> twin swarms of flutes'.
> 'Tamar, in your high breasts
> there are two fishes calling me
> and in your finger tips
> there are murmurs
> of an unopened rose'. (*CP* 36-6)

This passage again suggests that Webb opts for concision. 'My threads of blood' becomes 'My blood', 'light breezes' 'breezes'. And yet again, words and phrases which seem stilted in the Spender/Gili version are more satisfying in Webb's. His 'stop my eyes' is much more forceful and dramatic than the weak and rather polite 'efface these eyes', and 'unopened rose' is a more delicate and at the same time erotic evocation of Tamar's virginity than Spender and Gili's 'sealed rose', which almost suggests something never to be opened. It seems fair to say that Webb's version, if not perfect, reveals a much greater feeling for Lorca's original poem, as well as a greater directness.

In conclusion, Webb, like Vernon Watkins, was strongly attracted to the poetry of Lorca. The two poems translated by Watkins stemmed from his recognition in them of the theme of the loss of childhood innocence, the approach of a more difficult stage of life in adulthood, and in conjunction with it an awareness of the enigmatic nature of the world in which we find ourselves. Webb's ten translations also reflect a concern with the world of childhood in its varying aspects – wonder, fear, boldness –

and, perhaps, in 'Tamar and Amnon' a sense of the transition to the sexual instincts and even violence of adulthood. As well as this, though, both Webb and Watkins saw in Lorca's poetry, as well as in the work of other European poets, a universality which strengthened their own work and helped to broaden its terms of reference. The two Swansea poets were very different individuals in many ways, Watkins the non-Welsh speaking, non-political writer, Webb the Welsh-speaking nationalist and scourge of the English. But in certain respects they were clearly similar, and both were fine translators of Lorca.

NOTES

1 See Gwynne Edwards, 'Vernon Watkins, Dylan Thomas and the Poetry of Lorca', in Almanac, *Yearbook of Welsh Writing in English*, vol. 14 (Cardigan: Parthian, 2010), pp. 154-78.

2 Harri Webb, *A Militant Muse: Selected Literary Journalism 1948-80*, ed. Meic Stephens (Bridgend: Seren, 1998). See 'Webb's Progress (I)', p. 169.

3 See *Federico García Lorca: Gypsy Ballads/Romancero gitano*, trans. Robert Havard (Warminster: Aris and Phillips, 1990), p. 1.

4 Brian Morris, *Harri Webb* (Cardiff: University of Wales Press, 1993), p. 12.

5 Harri Webb, *A Militant Muse*. See 'Webb's Progress (II)', p. 198.

6 Brian Morris, *Harri Webb*, p. 57.

7 Harri Webb, *Collected Poems* ed. Meic Stephens (Llandysul: Gomer, 1995) p. 96. All further quotations from Webb's poems are from this edition and will be given in the text after the abbreviation CP. The poems in the collection retain Webb's punctuation or lack of it.

8 Ibid., p. 57.

9 See Don Dale-Jones, 'The Trouble with Harri: Some Thoughts on Two Writers for Our Time, Harri Webb (1920-1994) and T. Harri Jones (1921-1965)', in *Seeing Wales Whole. Essays*

on the Literature of Wales. In Honour of Meic Stephens, ed. Sam Adams (Cardiff: University of Wales Press, 1998), p. 75.

10 See Harri Webb, 'To the Young People of Wales', in *No Half-Way House. Selected Political Journalism*, ed. Meic Stephens (Talybont: Y Lolfa, 1997), p. 270.

11 M. Wynn Thomas, *Corresponding Cultures: the Two Literatures of Wales* (Cardiff: University of Wales Press, 1999), p. 54.

12 In a private telephone conversation.

13 See Ian Hilton, 'Vernon Watkins as Translator', in *Vernon Watkins* 1906-1967, ed. Leslie Norris (London: Faber and Faber, 1970), p. 83.

14 See *The Collected Poems of Vernon Watkins* (Ipswich: Golgonooza Press, 1986), p. 189.

15 See Gwynne Edwards, 'Vernon Watkins, Dylan Thomas and the Poetry of Lorca', op. cit., pp. 158, 164, 169, 176.

16 Meic Stephens in Harri Webb, *Collected Poems*, op. cit., p. 384.

17 Brian Morris, *Harri Webb*, p.14.

18 See G.G. Brown, *A Literary History of Spain. The Twentieth Century* (London: Ernest Benn, 1972), p. 86.

19 The works of Freud were published in Spain in Spanish translation from 1922 onwards and were eagerly read by, among others, Lorca, Salvador Dalí and Luis Buñuel when they were students at the Residencia de Estudiantes in Madrid in the early 1920s.

20 Federico García Lorca, *Lament for the Death of a Bullfighter and Other Poems in the Original Spanish*. With English Translation by A.L.Lloyd (London and Toronto: William Heinemann Ltd., 1937).

21 Federico García Lorca, *Poems*, translated by J.L. Gili and Stephen Spender (London: The Dolphin, 1939).

22 See Federico García Lorca, *Obras completas I, Poesía*, ed. Miguel García-Posada (Barcelona/Valencia: Galaxia Gutenberg/Círculo de Lectores, 1996), p. 416.

Old age in the fiction of Emyr Humphreys

Elinor Smith
Cardiff University

Like most developed countries, Wales has an ageing population. Given the ongoing rise in life expectancy and the falling national fertility rate, it is predicted that by 2026 30 percent of Welsh people will be over the age of sixty, compared to an estimated 24.6 percent in 2008, and that this figure will rise to more than 32 percent by 2046. The number of very old people is likely to increase greatly. The proportion of our population aged ninety and over will rise from less than one percent in 2008 to 3.4 percent by 2046[1]. That people are experiencing longer, healthier lives is undoubtedly a good thing, as are the developments in methods of and access to contraception which have enabled women to take greater control of their fertility over the last half century. However, the challenges presented by the ageing population are exercising government thinkers at a Welsh and a UK level. In 2008 the Welsh Assembly Government appointed an independent Older People's Commissioner to champion the particular concerns of senior citizens,[2] while last year the Conservative-Liberal Democrat coalition in Westminster announced plans to raise the state pension age earlier than envisaged previously in an attempt to 'better reflect changes in life expectancy'.[3]

Despite this recognition by politicians that the ageing population will have a significant impact on society as a whole, Western culture remains obsessed by the representations of youth which fixated it throughout the twentieth century[4]. Popular entertainment bombards us with images of teenage and twenty-something celebrities and advertisements for products which promise to delay or reverse the physical effects of ageing. Critics have identified various problems for older people in finding identities for themselves caused by this cultural preoccupation. Steven Katz suggests that marketing activities which connect 'the commodified values of youth with bodycare techniques for masking the appearance of age' can 'dissolve ... the significance of age ... in the fast-paced economies of images dominated by exercise, diet, cosmetic management and leisure activities' and also warns that positive discourses and images of age designed to address ageist stereotypes have inadvertently 'repressed important issues in old age'.[5] Mike Featherstone and Andrew Wernick warn that the 'long-standing' image of old age as a second childhood is an image of dependency which 'take[s] away the adult status and personhood of the elderly',[6] while Gerben J. Westerhof and Emmanuelle Tulle explain that older people are often under-represented and portrayed negatively in the media:

> Almost all studies on old people in the media have found that they are not well covered....Programmes are more often *about* older people than for older people and they seldom give older people their own voice.... Although there are minor variations according to the type of media and programmes, the percentage of older people in the mass media is well below their actual proportion in the general population.... Even when they are present, some studies have found that older characters are negatively portrayed, for example as asexual, incompetent or having health problems.[7]

This marginalisation of older people is ironic given that people in their eighties or nineties today have witnessed possibly the greatest social, political and cultural changes in any human lifetime. Events such as the introduction of universal suffrage in the United Kingdom, the Great Depression, and the Second World War are all still within living memory. Within Wales, the last ninety years have seen the country change from a rural and industrial society to a post-industrial economy and an about-turn in government policy on the Welsh language, yet the experiences of older people are less likely to receive attention than those of the young. Stereotypes also abound and tend to focus on concepts of physical and cognitive decay, incompetence and dependence.[8] It seems, then, that contemporary Western society, including Wales, is a difficult place in which to grow old.

Emyr Humphreys is ninety-one and has been a published novelist for more than sixty years. Perhaps unsurprisingly, he has written extensively about the experiences of older people during his own old age. His most recent collections of short stories, *Old People Are A Problem* (2003) and *The Woman at the Window* (2009), have centred on events in the lives of a variety of elderly characters. Earlier works have also examined aspects of ageing and intergenerational relationships. *Outside the House of Baal* (1965), for instance, is structured around the reminiscences of septuagenarian protagonists J.T. Miles and Kate Bannister (née Jones) intercut with episodes from their daily lives in the 1960s, while the 'Land of the Living' series of seven novels (1971-1991) charts the life of Amy Price Parry throughout the twentieth century. This essay examines representations of older people in a range of Emyr Humphreys's fiction. It discusses the depiction of the ageing body, alongside the representation of older people's knowledge and experience, their roles in society,[9] attitudes to the past and societal change, and the implications of the writer's use of humour. I hope that this exploration of a major Welsh novelist's engagement with old age will provide insight into the situation of older people in contemporary Welsh society and the challenges to them in establishing roles and identities for themselves.

Ageing bodies

Humphreys's representation of J.T. and Kate in the sections of Outside the *House of Baal* set in the 1960s foregrounds the effects of ageing on the body. The protagonists' advanced age is indicated through physical details in the descriptions which open the novel, for example in J.T.'s 'halo of white hair' and the information that he has trimmed his eyebrows,[10] and in Kate's 'stiff fingers' (18) and her 'intricately veined' though 'plump' cheeks (16). Both are described as having 'thin' arms (15/16), suggesting a loss of strength and resulting vulnerability. This sense of degeneration related to ageing is echoed in the pair's possessions, which have been worn by time and use. The tapes on Kate's faded pinafore are 'grey and frayed' (16), while the curtains in J.T.'s bedroom have 'washed thin' (15). The writer does not shy away from presenting the more intimate physical effects of ageing. As in other parts of the novel, his portraits of J.T and Kate include corporeal details such as the information that J.T has used his old-fashioned chamber pot 'twice during the night' and leaves a quantity of urine on the bathroom floor, presumably due to a loss of co-ordination. However, the precise and impersonal tone with which these occurrences are reported avoids prompting disgust or connoting stereotypes of 'smelly old people'. Instead, the effect is to promote empathy for the characters' experiences.

As the novel progresses, the reader is made aware of the increased physical effort which Kate and J.T. must make in their daily lives. For example, Kate is described as bending 'slowly' in the bathroom to pick up a towel before 'lower[ing] herself on to her knees', 'struggl[ing]' to reach the floorcloth and finally 'wringing it out with both hands until her fingers seemed to swell with the effort' (63). The precise detail with which the writer depicts Kate's actions in this and similar passages and the focus on the events of a single day in the chapters set in the 1960s contrast with the broad timescale and range of personal and historical events encompassed in the other, episodic parts of the novel. The effect of this distinction in the treatment of Kate and J.T.'s pasts and their present, aged existences is to emphasise the slowing down of their bodies with age.[11] The reader is sensitised to the physical care which the pair must take of themselves.

As well as illustrating the effects of ageing on the body, Humphreys explores the reactions of older characters to their changing physiques. A preoccupation with health and remaining fit is apparent in the text's older characters. J.T. is asked the name of his doctor by both Mr Ellis and Mr Bowen, indicating a shared interest in medical matters, and is described as stretching in front of a mirror when he gets up in the morning and 'knead[ing]' the flesh of his back 'like one who is determined to keep an upright carriage as long as he is able' (38). This response to the ageing of the body is also evident in Humphreys's later work. For example, in 'Home', a story from *The Woman at the Window*, the narrator Dilys explains that she takes a 'benevolent interest' in the gardener, Wil Hafan's health, 'which is his chief interest',[12] while in 'The Garden Cottage', Sir Robin Williams Price clearly worries about his physical condition: 'Much too conscious of my skeleton these days ... I suppose it comes from being so thin. It's all I've got left. The connection between my spine and my cortex' (194). The realism in the writer's representation of these anxieties about health is evident from Westerhof and Tulle's comments on the subject. The theorists explain that:

> [Studies...] have found that health and psychophysical functioning become more important aspects of self-concepts as people age. Not only do people complain more about problems in psychophysical functioning, such as reduced vitality and mobility, but they also construe their future more in terms of remaining healthy and maintaining fitness.[13]

Humphreys's older characters also appear dissatisfied with their aged appearances. To return to *Outside the House of Baal*, in chapter three, J.T and Kate both look at their reflections, he naked in a mirror in the bedroom and then in the bathroom as he shaves, she briefly in the window-pane as she looks outside. Kate is concerned both to avoid revealing her appearance to the milkboy and to avoid looking at it herself: 'She turned away quickly as if she were as eager not to see her image as to have it seen' (39). Similarly, whilst shaving J.T. 'screw[s] up his face as if he [is] examining it with some distaste' (40). The protagonists are also described observing their bodies in a detached way, as though they view them as somewhat separate from their conception of themselves. J.T. inspects the mole on his cheek with curiosity:

> It was an interesting shape and not unbecoming with a square, flat healthy-looking head. A benign growth a doctor once called it and ever since it had seemed a friendly object, although strange and inviting daily inspection (40-1).

As this action takes place in the bathroom, Kate is downstairs contemplating her elderly woman's hand and how it has changed since her wedding some forty years earlier:

> She looked down at the four fingers of her right hand pressed against the wood she herself had varnished brown three years ago. The wedding ring on her finger was out of all proportion, thick and heavy, and yet it could no longer be passed over the swollen knuckle. The skin of the hand was papery, but still womanly and not yet discoloured by extreme old age (39).

Although the narrative does not reveal Kate's thoughts directly, the reader sees the hand from her point of view and shares her observations. She is able to make an objective judgement on her body – that it is aged but 'still womanly' – and also to see its current state as part of a continuum of old age, the most extreme effects of which are yet to come. Bryan S. Turner explains that there is often a gap between the way that older people view themselves and the realities of their bodily situation:

> In phenomenological terms, we might note that the inside of the body remains subjectively young or youthful while the outside becomes both biologically and socially old. There is a necessary disjuncture between the inner self and the image of the body.[14]

Kate and J.T.'s distanced approach to their bodies and distaste for their appearance suggests that they are affected by such a disjuncture.

It is interesting that Kate refers to other characters as 'old', for example calling J.T. a 'soft old fool' (18) and Mr Hobley 'the old man' (182). She and J.T. are about the same age and Mr Hobley not necessarily any older – he fought in the First World War when J.T. was a stretcher-bearer. Again, social theories of ageing can help to interpret this behaviour; as Turner observes:

> We are resistant to the thought that we might become old, and have difficulty consequently forming an empathy for the aged even *when we are chronologically old*. In fact we might say that we find difficulty empathizing with our own process of ageing because we subjectively cling to an image of ourselves as unchangingly young.[15] (my italics)

Thus, it is possible that Kate has difficulty in perceiving her own ageing. This reading is supported by the capability and self sufficiency that the character exhibits, particularly in comparison to characters such as the vulnerable Mr Hobley, confused Dan Llew, or J.T. himself. Not only does Kate organise all three men, she runs the house practically single-handedly – it is she who is associated with work and action throughout the text, J.T. with thought and contemplation. Given this competence, it is unsurprising that she views herself as of a different age from those around her. However, the 'turn' (179) that she suffers as she busies herself with the housework and J.T.'s revelation that 'she does too much ... the doctor has warned her' (334) indicate that the disjunction between her inner perception of herself and her actual physical strength means she is pushing herself too hard.[16]

Like J.T. and Kate, the Countess Cecilia Von Leiden in *Unconditional Surrender* (1996) appears to feel detached from her older body and voices a dislike for her image, which suggests a gap between her perceived and physical selves. She refers to herself in the third person and in a dehumanising way at times, for example when she describes Colonel Bacon helping 'an arthritic old creature' into his car.[17] During the episode where she attempts to shoot the colonel, the countess looks at her 'dilapidated image in the dressing-table mirror' and 'loathe[s]' what she sees, calling it a 'mocking likeness' (143) of herself. However, Humphreys's presentation of Cecilia's relationship with her body is more complicated than that he employs for Kate and J.T. This complexity is aided by the novel's first-person narrative, which contrasts with the non-omniscient, third-person voice of *Outside the House of Baal*.[18] Through the passages narrated by Cecilia, the reader learns that she has a keen understanding of the way in which her aged appearance influences others' reactions to her. When considering how best to endear herself to Meg, the countess asks herself: 'Who would want to waste affection on a crumbling old hag like me?' (8). Later, she describes prisoner of war, Klaus 'staring at [her] as if [she] were an unidentified object retrieved from an excavated tomb' (23). These comments indicate her awareness of the tendency to devalue older people and view them as physically unpleasant and characterised by degeneration.

The very fact that it is Cecilia who perceives these preconceptions both reveals and undermines them in the eyes of the reader. The countess's ironic tone as she describes herself using stereotypes of decrepitude is also important as it serves to negate these assumptions by suggesting that she views herself as anything but a decayed being on the point of death.

Our view of Cecilia is complicated further by her actual age as, at fifty-seven, she could not be described as very old. One might suggest, therefore, that her being branded as 'old' has as much to do with her position as a German citizen 'marooned' (7) in Wales during and after the Second World War as with her actual needs. The placing of Cecilia in the Residential Home for Decayed Gentlewomen can be viewed as an attempt to suppress any threat which she might pose by both institutionalising her and labelling her 'old' and thus stereotypically weak and irrelevant. This interpretation is supported by the fact that, after the countess has caused embarrassment by getting drunk and discussing the state of the British Empire at the Gethin-Wynnes' party, Colonel Bacon begins to investigate her background, questions her right to be considered 'old' and consequently harmless, and looks for opportunities to return her to post-war Germany:

> The fact is, my dear chap, the old bird's got a record. Not so old as that either. A mere fifty-seven. As a matter of interest, is there an age limit of any kind for getting into the Residence? (79)

Knowledge and experience

Although the physical discomforts of ageing – often viewed as one of the more negative aspects of growing old[19] – and their effects on individual identity are presented in detail in *Outside the House of Baal* and *Unconditional Surrender*, I do not wish to imply that the impression of later life given by Humphreys in these texts is wholly negative. Both works create a sense that their older characters have built up a wealth of knowledge and experience throughout their lives, which is reminiscent of the figure of the wise old man or woman which one would find in literature and folk tales from the past. Cecilia appears to know herself well and is honest about and accepting of her failings. Recounting her visit to the Gethin-Wynnes, she comments: 'I snapped and surprised myself by sounding ungracious. Charm costs nothing. On the other hand I never had much to spare'(67). In *Outside the House of Baal*, J.T. and Kate's life experience is signified through possessions collected over time and imbued with memory and meaning. J.T. has reminders of his career – his books of handwritten sermons and old diaries – and still wears the winged collars which he chose over clerical ones for reasons of integrity half a century ago. In *Unconditional Surrender*, Cecilia also has possessions which are linked with her past life, in her case the jewels which she took with her when she left Germany and her first husband. This treasure comes to symbolise more than just its monetary value. The countess longs to give it to Meg to help her achieve 'independence' and 'freedom' (15), implicitly from the feeling of being trapped in an unhappy marriage which the older woman has experienced. In the same way, she wishes to pass on the knowledge she has gained through the events of her lifetime to help Meg avoid making similar mistakes:

> Klaus says this and Griff says that. It was so easy to imagine them both vying for her attention. That would give her a certain power. It was important for her to learn how to use it. If she were too trusting and innocent she would be more likely to suffer. These were the eternal truths I had to find a way of imparting to her without giving offence (89).

Similarly, J.T. has knowledge gained through his experience of bringing up a family which he can share with others, and tries to do so in an episode with a small child and its mother on the beach:

> – Don't, he said. You'll only be sorry. I remember once I was very angry with my daughter...
>
> – You mind your own bloody business, the woman said. And I'll mind mine...
>
> – The impressions that are made on them when they're small, J.T. said. You know these impressions are huge and last for life.
>
> – Look, she said. If you go on, I'll call the police and I'll file a complaint (391).

However, in both cases the older characters are unable to influence events as they wish. Cecilia chooses not to express her concerns for fear of causing Meg offence, and J.T.'s suggestions are met with threats. The elderly characters' failure to share the benefits of their knowledge raises questions about the ability of people of different ages to communicate across the generational divide, the roles which older people are able to play and the experiences that are open to them in a society where they are often undervalued.

What roles for older people?

In his recent short fiction, Humphreys focuses less on the physical aspects of the ageing process and its effects on individual identities than in the earlier texts discussed. This can be attributed in part to the different opportunities presented by the novel and story forms. For example, short stories do not offer the space for the kind of accumulation of precise descriptions of characters' domestic activities that the writer employs in the parts of *Outside the House of Baal* concerned with Kate and J.T.'s old age. Instead, in *Old People Are A Problem* and *The Woman at the Window*, the cumulative effect of the various presentations of older characters who populate the stories is to provide a multifaceted vision of what it is to be old in the early twenty-first century, where bodily change is only one of a variety of themes and concerns. One might suggest that, as well as resulting from differences in form, this widening of focus has come with Humphreys's firsthand experience of the ageing process. Though his presentation of physical ageing in *Outside the House of Baal* is subtle and sensitive, the writer was influenced by observing the experiences and recollections of his elderly mother and father-in-law when writing this work, rather than his own. What cannot be doubted is the diverse range of presentations of older individuals which the two collections of short stories offer for analysis, in particular for a consideration of the roles and experiences which the writer suggests are open to or typical of older people in contemporary society.

A number of Humphreys's short stories include older characters who have been written off as no longer of relevance to contemporary society. 'The Ring and the Book' is set in the upmarket Riviera Residential Home for the Elderly, where the management's main priority appears to be to avoid unnecessary work caused by complications relating to the residents. When Raymond mentions that he thinks he knows the confused inmate known as 'Millie', the director's assistant remarks 'How interesting', but 'the tone of voice also suggested how potentially awkward' (176). Millie's real name is Meleri, but she has been renamed by the employees of the residence. This act suggests that the staff do not see her as an individual, do not respect her enough to learn her real name and place no value on the past life of which it is a part:

> We think she is very well connected. I know she has a title. Lady something. She was here before I arrived. We call her 'Millie' and she seems to like it. After all we are all the same in the end, aren't we? (176).

The elderly lady is kept under control by patronising

cajoling more suited to children than adults:

> Millie, dear. It will be eating time soon. Let's get back to our rooms, shall we? There's a lovely programme on the television. All about red squirrels. You know how you love them (178).

Westerhof and Tulle describe this type of language as 'over accommodation' and 'elderspeak'. They explain its characteristics and origins:

> This kind of communicative style is characterised by a high pitch, overly prone intonation, loud voice, the use of concrete and familiar words, an easy grammar, and a directive and childish way of speaking, such as the use of 'we' when referring to an individual.... Patronising interaction is mediated by negative stereotypes of older people being incompetent or having sensory decrements.... It is mostly motivated by a wish to make an impression of nurturance and support, but it may also be related to motives of staying in control.

The extent to which Millie's concerns and past experiences have been dispensed with since entering the home is evident in that no one seems to have noticed the names inscribed in the ring which she treasures or to have asked her the story behind it. The pathos in her situation is also heightened by an awareness that she *is* frail and *does* need support of some kind, and that the nurses appear genuinely affectionate towards her. However, the treatment she receives seems to be grounded in the image of old age as a second childhood, devoid of independence and adult status, which Featherstone and Wernick have identified and is discussed above. Thus, the solution that has been offered for her need for care is not allowing her to be the adult person she has spent her life developing into.

Isolation, loss and the idea that the world has changed

too quickly for some older people to adjust to it feature in stories such as 'The Garden Cottage'. Sir Robin Williams Price is very excited to be hosting visitors Anna and Idris, suggesting his loneliness. He wants to hear everything about the couple's life, urging them to 'tell [him] all' (190/191) more than once and getting carried away with his own reminiscences before checking himself with an apologetic '[i]t's so good of you to listen to me' (198). It becomes apparent that the elderly man is gaining vicarious pleasure from his guests' tales of their family and upwardly mobile lifestyle, which contrasts with his life, characterised as it has been by a gradual stripping away of possessions, people and respect which echoes the degeneration of his body. There is pathos in his awareness that his aristocratic heritage is part of an out-dated institution which no longer commands the respect it did, and his financial problems are indicative of his inability to adapt to changing circumstances:

> People still thought of themselves as 'well born' in those days. Of course bags of jewels don't last forever. The sixties blew all that sort of thing away, just after we were married. We weren't really equipped to deal with all the equalitarian pressure around. No education. We'd been brought up to believe we were the best by right of birth, which was rubbish of course. Nothing worse than impoverished country squires (195).

Close family ties are also a thing of the past for Sir Robin, as his daughters eventually turn against him, and his wife, Marcia, is very recently dead herself. It is little wonder, then, that the old man is reduced to living in his memories, as nothing that he once cared about is left: 'Awful isn't it? Old men dwell too much in the past. Well of course they do. There isn't anywhere much else they can go' (195).

Sir Robin is not the only one of Humphreys's older characters who is living in the past. In 'Old People are a

Problem', ninety-three-year-old Mary Keturah Parry is, in her nephew Mihangel Parry-Paylin's view, 'wedded to the past'. Indeed, she still keeps imperial currency on the mantelpiece nearly four decades after decimalisation and idealises a time which is beyond even her living memory, when the village chapel played host to popular ministers of the religious revival. She speaks of:

> ...John Jones's last sermon. My grandmother remembered it you know. The chapel was full to overflowing and they sang, she said, full of joy and thanksgiving for the blessing of holy eloquence. It all happened here. Those were the days ... Those were the days. They had something to sing about ... A better world inside these walls (17).

It is this inability to live in the present, alongside Mihangel's lack of concern for her views, which causes ructions between Keturah and her family. Immersed as she is in her vision of the chapel's former glory, she cannot see the realities of its present state, that its falling congregation and dilapidated building make change of some kind essential.

Despite the inclusion of some of the sadder and more negative aspects of ageing in the stories discussed so far, Humphreys's recent short fiction also includes many positive images of older people engaged in a diverse range of roles and activities. Lucy, the elderly narrator of 'Sisters', remains active in society and is engaged with contemporary issues. Despite having lost or been disappointed by those she loves and becomes attached to, she has continued to protest with sister Eira against the injustices they see around them and characterise as 'The Silent Plague' (149). Lucy and Eira have outlasted many of the younger activists and remained more faithful to their principles:

> In our own quiet way Eira and I became seasoned

> protesters. We were at it so long we saw student leaders of the most ardent and idealistic kind succumb to the power of the silent plague and start swimming up the only channels the superstructure left open, to greater wealth and importance. It didn't take all that many years for them to mutate (149).

This staying power might be attributed to the sisters' greater life experience and, as a result, a more realistic approach than the idealistic young people they campaign alongside.

Many of Humphreys's older characters refuse to be disregarded and side-lined, instead fighting back and confounding stereotypes. On first encountering Keturah Parry in 'Old People are a Problem', her situation looks similar to that of Millie in 'The Ring and the Book'. She is also dismissed as no longer of relevance by those around her and viewed as a 'problem' to be controlled because she can't remain in her own home. The character's refusal to move from the Soar chapel cottage is based on her belief that the younger people around her do not value the chapel's history – the revivalist ministers who preached there – and the importance it once held for the local community. Cantankerous, stubborn and overly concerned with the past as she is, the treatment which the older woman receives ranges from the dismissive to the brutal. Mihangel disregards her opinions as out of touch with the reality of the situation. When she locks herself in the chapel, he decides to leave her to 'stew in her own juice' (135), a decision which contributes to the elderly lady's eventual death. The alderman's friend, Ennis Taft, would go further. He dismisses Keturah's distress as symptomatic of a typical older person's illness and suggests that she is disposed of through institutionalisation:

> The poor old biddy... She must be suffering from senile dementia. There's only one thing to do, San Fihangel.

> Section her. Or whatever it is they call it. All they need to do is ask her a few questions. What's the name of the Prime Minister of New Zealand? What day is it the day after tomorrow? That sort of thing (38).

However, Keturah refuses to accept this treatment and locks herself in the chapel. Humphreys's use of humour in this story encourages the reader to rejoice in the elderly lady's actions and to support her. The comic description of her setting up camp 'for a long siege' (34) with her paraffin stove and chamber pot and the rudeness with which she treats everyone around her, even accusing local historian Dr Derwyn of worshipping the 'Golden Calf', 'English Calf' and 'Money Calf' (35), prompts a gleeful response from the reader to her refusal to be dominated.

Humour is used to similar effect in other stories. In 'Three Old Men', octogenarian school friends Tom Philips, Roderick Roberts and Peter Pritchard stumble upon a runaway prisoner whilst investigating prehistoric ruins. When Rod confronts him, the younger man does not judge the others as a threat, presumably dismissing them due to their old age and its associations with incompetence and vulnerability:

> 'A man with an Irish accent escaped from Presswood Open Prison three days ago. Or was it four.'
>
> The Irishman gave a deep sign and then a smile.
>
> 'The public are advised,' he said, 'to contact the police and not to approach him. Especially three old men' (216).

However, the convict has not counted on the old men still having their wits about them and being able to incapacitate him. Again, the comic elements of this episode extract a response of gleeful support from readers, making them complicit with the marginalised older characters and thus working against the 'Othering' of such individuals in popular discourse. Peter reinvents the trappings of old age when he hits the runaway with his walking stick and puts his years of experience in horror films to use with a theatrical groan. The younger man's reaction is suitably pathetic: 'You're a monster... I'm maimed for life' (216). Thus, through stories like 'Old People are a Problem' and 'Three Old Men', Humphreys critiques the dismissal of older people as no longer relevant, shows that some are not as weak and vulnerable as stereotypes suggest and moves the reader's perspective on the subject to become supporters of the so-called underdogs. Unfortunately, Keturah's actions are so extreme that they are bound to end badly. Without an amount of compromise from both her and those around her – she needs to take a more open approach to change, Mihangel needs to listen to her concerns – there seems to be no way out other than her eventual death.

In some cases, Humphreys's older characters are still learning and changing in old age, thus challenging perceptions of later life as a time of social and intellectual stasis or degeneration. With the death of her husband, Dilys in 'Home' initially seems at a loss. She has devoted her life to accompanying Dennis on his travels and is now in a position where her own identity and purpose seem unstable and, because of the incessant travelling, she has no place where she feels at home:

> Without him, everywhere becomes cold and hostile and foreign and I am like the proverbial pilgrim in a foreign land. None of his accomplishments were mine so what am I without him? (143).

The protagonist cannot turn to her family for company or purpose, as she has been separated emotionally and geographically from her son Daniel since she and Dennis sent him to boarding school and rarely sees her grandchildren. However, at the age of seventy-three, Dilys embarks on what Daniel describes as a 'new adventure'

(142) near to her father's birthplace of Gelliwen on Anglesey. Within months she has company and a role to play in the community. While local boy Cledwyn plays chess with Cyril, son of the Bulgarian daily help, as he recuperates in the bedroom Dilys had reserved for her absent grandson, the elderly lady sets about healing a rift between the boys' mothers. She also finds intellectual employment in preparing her father's papers for publication and concludes that she has begun to feel grounded and 'at home': 'Some kind of a household is forming, and in my own mind I can call Henefail, and the village and this ancient sprawling parish, home' (163).

Rather like the countess in *Unconditional Surrender* understanding the effects of her physical appearance, Elsie Probert, in 'Before the War', displays an appreciation of the value which she holds as an older person for her niece, Non, and uses it for her own benefit. Until embarking on her PhD, Non took little interest in Elsie. However, now that she is researching Welsh history, she hopes that the older lady will be a useful source of firsthand information on subjects such as 'social deprivation in the rural environment' and 'the arrival of piped water' (66). However, Elsie has her own need for information – a desire for news and gossip about the family. She decides to provide Non with what she needs only when the younger woman answers her questions: 'A qualified understanding had to be reached. The old woman would only talk freely if she were fed tit-bits of inside family information' (68). She also seems comfortable and realistic about the lifestage she has reached, as she is able to make jokes about her death, which, at eighty-six, is very likely to come in the next decade:

> 'It's fine, Auntie. Really I want you to say whatever you like.'
> 'Goodness knows what I'll say. Rambling on.'
> 'That's fine. We've got all the time in the world.'
> Non's anxiety to please amused her great aunt.
> 'Have I? That's nice to know' (56-7).

Thus, the character negotiates with and uses her position as an older person, rather than just accepting it unquestioningly.

Given their inclusion of both positive and negative experiences of later life and the broad range of roles played by elderly characters, Emyr Humphreys's short stories give an eclectic vision of old age which avoids reinforcing stereotypes, often confounds them and builds upon the sensitive portrayals in his earlier work. The mixing of positive and negative aspects of later life, often within a single story, also suggests that experiences of old age cannot be classified simplistically as either 'good' or 'bad'. It would go against any attempt to encourage realistic attitudes to and images of old age to provide only representations of the happy, fulfilled, active lifestyle promoted by some advertisements aimed at older people, as the challenges of ageing would then be denied rather than addressed. As discussed above, Katz has identified the efforts of some positive ageing groups as being in some ways counterproductive for this very reason. Most importantly, the variety and way in which characters engage with their own ageing – be it by prioritising fitness or manipulating others' expectations – and in some cases fight against attempts to stereotype or suppress them indicates that there are various possible ageing experiences and choices to be made by individuals old and young, and by wider society. Throughout his fiction, Humphreys avoids treating older people as a homogenous group with camaraderie in their shared age. At the end of 'Three Old Men', for example, Tom is disappointed that Rod and Peter are too tired and cross to celebrate their victory over the escaped prisoner and instead begin to argue about religion. Bemoaning the fact that he must take Rod home before he can escape to the soothing surroundings of his office, Tom reflects on the three men's relationship, suggesting that they are destined never to be close: 'Old age was not enough to share in common. Our lives had run parallel, but for the life of me I couldn't remember whether parallel lines met in infinity or not' (218). Similarly, there is no camaraderie in old age at the Residential Home for Decayed Gentlewomen in *Unconditional Surrender*, where the countess is subjected to racist treatment from her fellow residents.

One might feel concerned at Humphreys's extraction of humour from his representations of older people, as it could make them figures of fun or play on stereotypes such as those of mental deterioration and confusion. From the bathetic image of Kate in *Outside the House of Baal* searching furtively in a bowl of prunes for her glass eye and disposing of the evidence before J.T. finds out, to Sir Robin in 'The Garden Cottage' and his temporary loss of control over the humorously described 'masticating process', the indignities of old age are related to comic effect. However, as Mary-Ann Constantine puts it, Humphreys is 'even-handed in his teasing'.[23] So, the reader can find amusement in Ifan Roberts youthfully assuring his grandfather that his friendship with Zofia Worowski is in no way 'sentimental', but rather based on having 'all these interests in common' so that 'you could say it's just an accident that she happens to be a girl' ('A Little History'), in the same way that he or she can laugh at Keturah Parry's old pennies and peppermint cake. Also, humour often comes from the writer's ironically revealing common human mistakes and self-deceptions, rather than specifically elderly characteristics or actions. For example, although the twist at the end of 'The Grudge' hinges on elderly poet Gwilym Hesgyn suffering a stroke and being unable to recognise loved ones, including his daughter – a common illness and memory problem in older people, it is not the illness or forgetfulness which the reader finds amusement in. Rather, the bitter humour which comes with Gwilym's apparently happy recognition of his cousin Lord Clement Parry is derived from the speed with which the pair's long-running disagreement is forgotten and the irony that the only person the poet recognises is the man he has obsessively disliked and competed with since childhood. The 'rigid diagonal smile' which is 'fixed' (30) on Gwilym's face might also be read as an effect of the stroke rather than a reaction to Lord Parry's presence, suggesting that the poet is doomed to be fussed over by a man he can't stand and providing a humorous comeuppance for his haranguing his daughter about the grudge and other irritations.

The complex vision of old age found in Emyr Humphreys's fiction can be seen as a positive contribution to the representation of older people in cultural discourse. The writer does a great deal to encourage an empathetic response from the reader to his elderly characters. The detailed and sensitive depiction of the effects of ageing on the body and the frustrations and health concerns that come with it in *Outside the House of Baal* promotes understanding in the reader. Similarly, the representation across Humphreys's novels and short stories of senior citizens who are dismissed, disregarded and de-individualised by those around them encourages sympathy and increased awareness of the isolation which characterises the lives of some older people. The writer's presentation of older characters also works against the tendency to stereotype the elderly. Cecilia in *Unconditional Surrender* is astute enough to detect and ironise the preconceptions which people have of her, thus contradicting the stereotype of older people as mentally deficient, while Keturah Parry and the protagonists in 'Three Old Men' negate stereotypes of vulnerability by fighting back against those who try to dominate them. The use of humour is important in these depictions, as it encourages the reader to support older characters and revel in their successes. Stereotyping is also discouraged through the sheer variety of experiences of old age contained in Humphreys's work. On the whole the reader is encouraged to conclude that old age does not have to mean obsolescence. Many of the writer's depictions of older people involve a strong sense of their wealth of knowledge and experience. Characters such as Cecilia and Elsie Probert exhibit an understanding of human relationships and good judgement grounded in decades of life experience. Although, in some of the stories, older individuals have so little to enjoy in the present that they have retreated into the past, characters such as Dilys in 'Home' and Lucy in 'Sisters' are still changing, learning and contributing to society despite their advanced age.

NOTES

This essay is based on a longer MA thesis. ''The things that have happened in our time': Old age in the fiction of Emyr Humphreys', which is available at Cardiff University, Arts and Social Sciences Library.

1 Percentages calculated using data from Steve Rowan ed., *National Population Projections 2008-based* (Series PP2 No 27) (Office of National Statistics, 2008).
2 Martin Shipton, 'Wales appoints older people champion', *Western Mail*, 7 January 2008, available at: www.walesonline.co.uk/news/wales-news/2008/01/07/wales-appoints-older-people-champion-91466-20319139/ (accessed 22 January, 2011).
3 Allegra Stratton, 'Retirement age rise plan attacked by charities and unions', *guardian.co.uk*, 24 June 2010, available at: www.guardian.co.uk/money/2010/jun/24/state-pension-age-rise-plan (accessed 22 January, 2011).
4 Featherstone and Wernick link this valuing of youth over maturity to modern capitalist economics: 'Capitalist industrialization, with its continually revamped technologies of production also led to the transformation of domestic production and consumption. It idealized youth (including the eroticized youthful female body as the universal

consumer image of desirability) while fundamentally weakening the value of accumulated life experience, both in itself and as a marker of social status ... The work society with its loss of function and income which came with mandatory retirement became bolstered by a consumer culture with its images of youth fitness and beauty lifestyles which produced a new set of exclusions for older people.' Mike Featherstone and Andrew Wernick, 'Introduction', in *Images of Aging: Cultural representations of later life*, ed. Mike Featherstone and Andrew Wernick (London and New York: Routledge, 1995), pp. 1-15, p. 7.

5 Steven Katz, 'Imagining the life-span: From premodern miracles to postmodern fantasies', in *Images of Aging: Cultural representations of later life*, ed. Mike Featherstone and Andrew Wernick (London and New York: Routledge, 1995), pp. 61-75, p. 70.

6 Featherstone and Wernick, 'Introduction', p. 7.

7 Gerben J. Westerhof and Emmanuelle Tulle, 'Meanings of ageing and old age: discursive contexts, social attitudes and personal identities', in *Ageing in Society*, 3rd edn., ed. John Bond, Sheila Peace, Freya Dittman-Kohli and Gerben J. Westerhof (London, Los Angeles, New Delhi and Singapore: Sage Publications, 2007), pp. 235-254, p. 241.

8 Sara Munson Deats and Lagretta Tallent Lenker discuss the stereotyping of elderly people, including the 'traditional portrait of old age as a time of infirmity and senility' and 'the weak face of deterioration and decline traditionally depicted by the medical profession'. See Sara Munson Deats and Lagretta Tallent Lenker, 'Introduction', in *Aging and Identity: A Humanities Perspective*, ed. Sara Munson Deats and Lagretta Tallent Lenker (Westport, Connecticut: Praeger Publishers, 1999), pp. 1-20, p.3. For a discussion of recent social research into stereotypes of older people, see pp. 245-8 of Westerhof and Tulle, 'Meanings of ageing and old age'.

9 Older people in Humphreys's novels also have an important role as guardians of the Welsh cultural and linguistic inheritances, which they are sometimes able to pass on to

younger generations. A full exploration of this important aspect of Humphreys' work is beyond the scope of this essay; it is further explored in my MA thesis, '"The things that have happened in our time': Old age in the fiction of Emyr Humphreys'.

10 Emyr Humphreys, *Outside the House of Baal* (Bridgend: Seren, 1996), p. 15. All further references are to this edition and are given parenthetically in the text.

11 Thomas discusses Humphreys's management of time in *Outside the House of Baal* and states that the writer is successful in 'distinguishing between the pace of living during youth and vigorous prime, and the slowing down, not only of physical movement, but of the very metabolism (so to speak) of consciousness itself, that is part of the ageing process'. See M. Wynn Thomas, 'Outside the House of Baal: The Evolution of a Major Novel', in *Seeing Wales Whole*, ed. Sam Adams (Cardiff: University of Wales Press, 1998), pp. 121-143, p. 131.

12 Emyr Humphreys, *The Woman at the Window* (Bridgend: Seren, 2009), p. 153. All further references are to this edition and are given parenthetically in the text.

13 Westerhof and Tulle, 'Meanings of ageing and old age', p. 249.

14 Bryan S. Turner, 'Aging and identity: Some reflections on the somatisation of the self', in *Images of Aging: Cultural representations of later life*, ed. Mike Featherstone and Andrew Wernick (London and New York: Routledge, 1995), pp. 245-260, p. 250.

15 Turner, 'Aging and identity', pp. 249-50.

16 Jeremy Hooker writes of Kate and J.T.: 'She is the realist who does good practically, and a truthteller; J.T. is the idealist, the theorist of doing good practically, who often does it impractically.' Jeremy Hooker, 'Emyr Humphreys: A Seeing Belief', in *The Poetry of Place: Essays and Reviews 1970-1981* (Manchester: Carcanet Press, 1982), pp. 93-105.

17 Emyr Humphreys, *Unconditional Surrender* (1996), (Bridgend: Seren, 1997), p. 20. All further references are to

this edition and are given parenthetically in the text.

18 For a discussion of the strengths of the impartial, observational narration of *Outside the House of Baal*, in particular the ambivalence of its attitude to the actions described, see Thomas, 'Outside the House of Baal: The Evolution of a Major Novel'.

19 Westerhof and Tulle outline the findings of Dutch and American studies into the views of older people on the positive and negative aspects of the ageing experience: 'Positive aspects were mainly found in the social domain (e.g. freedom, fewer responsibilities, respect, relationships with grandchildren) and the psychological domain (e.g. life experience, wisdom, inner calmness), whereas negative aspects of one's own ageing process were found in the physical domain (e.g. losses of psychophysical functioning, vitality, mobility, strength, as well as changes in appearance) and in the social domain (e.g. attrition in one's social position, losses in personal relationships and loss of independence).' Westerhof and Tulle, 'Meanings of ageing and old age', pp. 248-9.

20 For Humphreys's discussion of the 'gift' of living with his elderly mother and father-in-law whilst both were in their seventies see Emyr Humphreys, 'Preface', in *Outside the House of Baal* (1965), (Bridgend: Seren, 1996), pp. 7-13.

21 Westerhof and Tulle, 'Meanings of ageing and old age', p. 246.

22 Emyr Humphreys, *Old People are a Problem*, (2003), (Bridgend: Seren, 2003), p. 11. All further references are to this edition and are given parenthetically in the text.

23 Mary-Ann Constantine, Review of *The Woman at the Window, New Welsh Review*, 86 (2009), pp. 73-4, p. 74.

Welsh Writing in English: A bibliography of criticism 2009

Laura Wainwright
Cardiff University

This bibliography covers books, contributions to books, periodical articles, review-articles, reviews of listed critical writing and selected theses. Readers aware of relevant material published in 2009, which has been omitted, are kindly asked to forward details to the Editor, *Almanac – Yearbook of Welsh Writing in English*, School of English Communication and Philosophy, Cardiff University, CF10 3EU.

GENERAL CRITICISM

Adams, Sam. Letter from Wales. *PN Review* 35/4 (March/April 2009) 8-10. ISSN 01447076. (Notes the achievements of Meic Stephens and Tony Conran, and discusses work by Robert Minhinnick and Graham Hartill).

Adams, Sam. Letter from Wales. *PN Review* 35/5 (May/June 2009) 6-8. ISSN 01447076. (Considers the Herbert family name in the context of Welsh literature and culture).

Ballin, Malcolm. Quite Healthy with Inbreeding? *New Welsh Review* 84 (Summer 2009) 9-17. ISSN 09542116. (On the 21-year history of the *New Welsh Review*).

Connolly, Claire and Katie Gramich (editors). *Irish Studies Review* 7/1 (2009). Special Issue: Irish and Welsh Writing. ISSN 14699303 (electronic) 09670882 (paper). Contents: Introduction, by Claire Connolly and Katie Gramich, pp.1-

4 – Public intellectuals, language revival and cultural nationalism in Ireland and Wales: a comparison of Douglas Hyde and Saunders Lewis, by Paul O'Leary, pp.5-18 – Creating and destroying 'the man who does not exist': the peasantry and modernity in Welsh and Irish writing, by Katie Gramich, pp.19-30 – Borderlands: spiritualism and the occult in *fin de siècle* and Edwardian Welsh and Irish horror, by Darryl Jones, pp.31-44 – The Irish Dylan Thomas: versions and influences, by Terence Brown, pp.45-54 – Foras na Gaeilge and Bwrdd yr Iaith Gymraeg: yoked but not yet shackled, by Colin H. Williams, pp.55-88 – Another lost cause? Pan-Celticism, race and language, by Daniel G. Williams, pp.89-101 – Speculating: Patrick McGuinness interviews Paul Muldoon, Interview by Patrick McGuinness, pp.103-110 – Y Gal, by Dafydd ap Gwilym, pp.111-113 – Reviews, by Valerie McGowen Doyle, Brad Kent, Claire Fitzpatrick; Will May; Eva Urban, Claire V. Nally; Neal Alexander, Eamon Maher, Laura Wainwright, pp.115-133.

Gramich, Katie (editor). *Almanac – Yearbook of Welsh Writing in English: Critical Essays* 14 (2009-10). ISBN 978-1905762781. Contents: Civilizing the Natives: Henry M. Stanley's and Joseph Conrad's Narratives of Identity, by Steve Hendon, pp.1-35 – 'Winding Silkworms' cocoons without a reel: Betsy Cadwaladyr, Jane Williams (Ystafell) and the Writing of the Autobiography of Elizabeth Davis, by Gwyneth Tyson Roberts, pp.36-61 – Original Preface to the Autobiography of Elizabeth Davis, by Jane Williams (Ystafell), pp.62-64 – Visions of Wales: *The Welsh Outlook*, 1914-1933, by Alyce von Rothkirch, pp.65-92 – Spaces of International Comparison in Welsh Periodicals in English, 1882-2008, by Malcolm Ballin, pp.93-120 – Exact Mystery: Some Aspects of Vernon Watkins's Poetics, by John Powell Ward, pp.121-153 – Vernon Watkins, Dylan Thomas and the Poetry of Lorca, by Gwynne Edwards, pp.154-178 – Defamiliarising Idris Davies: A

Reassessment of *Gwalia Deserta* and 'Gwalia My Song', by Alan Vaughan Jones, pp.179-207 – Hugh MacDiarmid and Keidrych Rhys: The Arrow from Wales, by Hugh Manson, pp.208-213 – The Burial of T. J. Llewelyn Prichard: An Addendum to a Note Concerning the Finding of a Prichard Manuscript, by Sam Adams, pp.214-220 – Welsh Writing in English: a bibliography of criticism 2009, compiled by Catherine Phelps, pp.222-237.

Jarvis, Matthew. A Poetry of Diversification: New Voices of the 1970s. *Poetry Wales* 44/3 (Winter 2008/2009) 43-48. ISSN 03322202.

Jarvis, Matthew. Divergent Paths: Poetic Divisions in the 1990s. *Poetry Wales* 45/1 (Summer 2009) 29-36. ISSN 03322202.

Jarvis, Matthew. Energies of Commitment: Poetry and Politics in the 1980s. *Poetry Wales* 44/4 (Spring 2009) 11-16. ISSN 03322202.

Jarvis, Matthew and John Kinsella. Welsh Environments: a Dialogue. *Poetry Wales* 45/2 (Autumn 2009) 39-44. ISSN 03322202. (Considers the issues raised by Matthew Jarvis's critical study, *Welsh Environments in Contemporary Poetry*, published by University of Wales Press in 2008).

Jones, Huw David. 'War Declared': Art and Society in Wales, 1969-77. *Planet: The Welsh Internationalist* 196 (Autumn 2009) 47-56. ISSN 00484288.

Jones, John Sam. Out of hearsay. *New Welsh Review* 83 (Spring 2009) 33-38. ISSN 09542116. (Reflects on writing from Wales by gay and lesbian authors).

Keenoy, Ray, Rhian Reynolds and Sioned Puw Rowlands (editors). *The Babel Guide to Welsh Fiction*. Oxford:

Boulevard Books, 2009. ISBN 9780708321911.

Minhinnick, Robert. 1147 and all that: or The Triban's Visitation. *Poetry Wales* 45/2 (Autumn 2009) 27-31. ISSN 03322202. (On literary culture in the Llynfi Valley).

Roberts, Harri Garrod. *Embodying Identity: Representations of the Body in Welsh Literature*. Cardiff: University of Wales Press, 2009. ISBN 978-0-7083-2169-0.

Roberts Jones, Sally. London and the Second Flowering. *Planet: The Welsh Internationalist* 194 (Spring 2009) 67-72. ISSN 00484288. (On Welsh writing in London in the 1960s).

Stephens, Meic. A farewell to English. *PN Review* 35/4 (March/April 2009) 50-53. ISSN 01447076 (On Welsh-language poets whose first language is English).

Stradling, Robert. "We knew Len...". *Planet: The Welsh Internationalist* 193 (February/March 2009) 49-55. ISSN 00484288. (On Welsh writing in English and the Spanish Civil War).

INDIVIDUAL AUTHORS

Dannie Abse

Archard, Cary. The power of translation: the influence of Rilke on Alun Lewis and Dannie Abse. *Agenda* 44/2-3 (2009) 113-117. ISSN 00020796.

Betsy Cadwaladyr

Tyson Roberts, Gwyneth. 'Winding Silkworms' cocoons without a reel: Betsy Cadwaladyr, Jane Williams (Ysgafell) and the Writing of the Autobiography of Elizabeth Davis.

Almanac – Yearbook of Welsh Writing in English: Critical Essays 14 (2009-10) 36-61.

Williams (Ysgafell), Jane. Original Preface to the Autobiography of Elizabeth Davis. *Almanac – Yearbook of Welsh Writing in English: Critical Essays* 14 (2009-10) 62-64.

GILLIAN CLARKE

McCarthy, Patricia. Patricia McCarthy interviews Gillian Clarke. *Agenda* 44/2-3 (2009) 127-150. (Interview). ISSN 00020796.

Tony Conran

Adams, Sam. Letter from Wales. *PN Review* 35/4 (March/April 2009) 8-10. ISSN 01447076. (Considers the achievements of Meic Stephens and Tony Conran, and discusses work by Robert Minhinnick and Graham Hartill).

John Cowper Powys

Dunn, John. The missing woman and John Cowper Powys's political philosophy. *Powys Journal* 19 (2009) 55-78. ISSN 09627057.

Holm Aagard, Jonas. John Cowper Powys: titles. *Powys Journal* 19 (2009) 127-150. ISSN 09627057.

Keith, W. J. John Cowper Powys and 'other dimensions': the evidence from his fiction. *Powys Journal* 19 (2009) 36-54. ISSN 09627057.

Marie-Laverrou, Florence. *A Glastonbury Romance* de John Cowper Powys: mortifères ressassements ou fécondes remémorations? *Études Britanniques Contemporaines* 36

(2009) 1-18. ISSN 11684917.

Mulder, Arjen. Becoming John Cowper Powys: on the four early novels. Powys Journal 19 (2009) 24-35. ISSN 09627057.

Reichmann, Angelika. In love with the abject: John Cowper Powys's Weymouth Sands. *Powys Journal* 19 (2009) 79-106. ISSN 09627057.

Idris Davies

Vaughan Jones, Alan. Defamiliarising Idris Davies: A Reassessment of *Gwalia Deserta* and 'Gwalia My Song'. *Almanac – Yearbook of Welsh Writing in English: Critical Essays* 14 (2009-10) 179-207.

Rhys Davies

Osborne, Huw. *Rhys Davies*. Writers of Wales Series. Cardiff: University of Wales Press, 2009. ISBN 9780708321676.

Russell T. Davies

Cranny-Francis, Anne. Why the Cybermen Stomp: Sound in the New *Doctor Who*. *Mosaic: A Journal for the Interdisciplinary Study of Literature* 42/2 (June 2009) 119-134. ISSN 00271276.

Niall Griffiths

Keyes, Jarrad. 'Archaeologies of the Future?': Niall Griffiths – Pathways of the Urban. *The Idea of the City: Early-Modern, Modern and Post-Modern Locations and Communities*. Joan Fitzpatrick (editor). Newcastle upon Tyne: Cambridge Scholars Press, 2009. pp.133-143. ISBN

9781443801461.

Graham Hartill

Adams, Sam. Letter from Wales. *PN Review* 35/4 (March/April 2009) 8-10. ISSN 01447076. (Considers the achievements of Meic Stephens and Tony Conran, and discusses work by Robert Minhinnick and Graham Hartill).

Felicia Hemans

Comet, Noah. Felicia Hemans and the 'Exquisite Remains' of *Modern Greece*. *Keats-Shelley Journal: Keats, Shelley, Byron, Hunt, and Their Circles* 58 (2009) 96-113. ISSN 04534387.

Dabundo, Laura. Wales and the Romantic Imagination/ Claiming Cambria: Invoking the Welsh in the Romantic Era. *Wordsworth Circle* 40/4 (Autumn 2009) 173-174. ISSN 00438006.

Esterhammer, Angela. Translating the Elgin Marbles: Byron, Hemans, Keats. *Wordsworth Circle* 40/1 (Winter 2009) 29-36. ISSN 00438006.

Hessell, Nikki. Romantic Literature and Indigenous Languages: Reading Felicia Hemans in Te Reo Maori. *European Romantic Review* 20/2 (April 2009) 261-270. ISSN 10509585.

Mason, Emma and Jonathan Roberts. Felicia Hemans's *Sonnets on Female Characters of Scripture*. *Yearbook of English Studies* 39/1-2 (2009) 72-83. ISSN 03062473.

Melnyk, Julie. William Wordsworth and Felicia Hemans. *Fellow Romantics: Male and Female British Writers*, 1790-1835. Beth Lau (editor). Farnham, Surrey: Ashgate, 2009.

pp. 139-158. ISBN 9780754663539.

O'Neill, Michael. 'A deeper and richer music': Felicia Hemans in dialogue with Wordsworth, Byron and Shelley. *Charles Lamb Bulletin* 145 (2009) 3-12. ISSN 03080951.

George Herbert

Adrian, John M. George Herbert, parish 'dexterity', and the local modification of Laudianism. *The Seventeenth Century* 24/1 (April 2009) 26-51. ISSN 0268117X.

Christensen, Philip Harlan. Herbert's 'Peace'. *The Explicator* 67/2 (Winter, 2009) 105-108. ISSN 00144140.

Davies Michael, Jennifer. Silence and 'Wounded Speech' in George Herbert's Poetry. *Sewanee Theological Review* 52/4 (2009) 343-364. ISSN 10599576.

Kinney, Arthur F. George Herbert's Early Readers. *Ben Jonson Journal: Literary Contexts in the Age of Elizabeth, James and Charles* 16/1-2 (May 2009) 77-98. ISSN 10793453.

Sheldrake, Philip (editor). *Heaven in Ordinary: George Herbert and his Writings*. Norwich: Canterbury Press, 2009. ISBN 978-1853119484.

Emyr Humphreys

Diane Green. *Emyr Humphreys: A Postcolonial Novelist?* Cardiff: University of Wales Press, 2009. ISBN 978-0-7083-2217-8.

John James

Williams, Nerys. Chronicling the half-life of poetry: Robert Minhinnick, Gwyneth Lewis and John James's longer poems. *Poetry Wales* 45/3 (Winter 2009/2010) 43-49. ISSN 03322202.

David Jones

Matthews, Steven. Provincialism and the Modern Diaspora: T. S. Eliot and David Jones. *English: The Journal of the English Association* (Spring 2009) 57-72. ISSN 00138215.

Smith-Long, Tim. 'My Greek Sailors speak Cockney': the principle of abstraction in the works of David Jones. *Agenda* 44/ 2-3 (2009) 81-92. ISSN 00020796.

Lewis Jones

del Valle Alcalá, Roberto. Rising with one's community: socialist theory and bildungsroman in Lewis Jones. *Cultura, Languaje y Representacíon/ Culture, Language and Representation* 7 (2009) 141-155. ISSN 16977750.

Richard Llewellyn

Adams, Sam. *Letter from Wales*. PN Review 35/6 (July/August 2009) 7-9. ISSN 01447076. (On Llewellyn's 1939 novel, How Green Was My Valley).

T. J. Llewelyn Prichard

Adams, Sam. The Burial of T. J. Llewelyn Prichard: An Addendum to a Note Concerning the Finding of a Prichard Manuscript. *Almanac – Yearbook of Welsh Writing in English: Critical Essays* 14 (2009-10) 214-220.

Alun Lewis

Archard, Cary. The power of translation: the influence of Rilke on Alun Lewis and Dannie Abse. *Agenda* 44/2-3 (2009) 113-117. ISSN 00020796.

Eiluned Lewis

MacNamee, Jane. Darkness and Light. *New Welsh Review* 83 (Spring 2009) 17-24. ISSN 09542116. (A discussion of the life and work of Eiluned Lewis with her daughter, Katrina Burnett).

Gwyneth Lewis

Brigley Thompson, Zoë. 'The Life and Death of Language': A Kristevan Reading of the Poets Gwyneth Lewis and Mebh McGuchian. *Orbis Litterarum: International Review of Literary Studies* 64/5 (2009) 385-412. ISSN 01057510.

Entwistle, Alice. 'A Kind of Authentic Lie': Authenticity and the Lyric Sequence in Gwyneth Lewis's English-Language Poetry. *Life Writing* 6/1 (April 2009) 27-43. ISSN 14484528.

Williams, Nerys. Chronicling the half-life of poetry: Robert Minhinnick, Gwyneth Lewis and John James's longer poems. *Poetry Wales* 45/3 (Winter 2009/2010) 43-49. ISSN 03322202.

THE MABINOGION AND RELATED MATERIALS

Adams, David. The Monks of Abergavenny: Rewriting Welsh Theatre History. *Planet: The Welsh Internationalist* 193 (February/March 2009) 60-65. ISSN 00484288. (On medieval theatre).

Cichon, Michael. *Violence and Vengeance in Middle Welsh and English Narrative: Owein and Ywain and Gawain*. Lewiston NY; Lampeter: Mellen Press, 2009. ISBN 0773446583.

Tolstoy, Nikolai. *Oldest British Prose Literature: The Compilation of the Four Branches of the Mabinogi*. Llanbedr: The Edwin Mellen Press, 2009. ISBN 9780773447103.

Arthur Machen

Lebbon, Tim. More in the Journey. *New Welsh Review* 84 (Summer, 2009) 18-24. ISSN 09542116.

Roland Mathias

Hooker, Jeremy. For Roland Mathias: tribute and apology. *Scintilla 13* (2009) 95-100. Reference number: 2009:15721.

Robert Minhinnick

Adams, Sam. Letter from Wales. *PN Revi*ew 35/4 (March/April 2009) 8-10. ISSN 01447076. (Considers the achievements of Meic Stephens and Tony Conran, and discusses work by Robert Minhinnick and Graham Hartill).

Williams, Nerys. Chronicling the half-life of poetry: Robert Minhinnick, Gwyneth Lewis and John James's longer poems. *Poetry Wales* 45/3 (Winter 2009/2010) 43-49. ISSN 03322202.

Katherine Philips

Gray, Catherine. Katherine Philips in Ireland. *English Literary Renaissance* 39/3 (Autumn 2009) 557-585. ISSN 00138312.

Prescott, Sarah. Archipelagic Orinda? Katherine Philips and the writing of Welsh women's literary history. *Literature Compass* 6/6 (2009) 1167-1176. Reference number: 2009:7190.

Keidrych Rhys

Manson, Hugh. Hugh MacDiarmid and Keidrych Rhys: The Arrow from Wales. *Almanac – Yearbook of Welsh Writing in English: Critical Essays* 14 (2009-10) 208-213.

Lynette Roberts

McGuinness, Patrick. Machine-age Mabinogion – 'A quite extraordinary affair': the impetuous and free-ranging work of Lynette Roberts. *Times Literary Supplement* 5562 (November 6 2009) 14-15.

Sheers, Owen. *A Poet's Guide to Britain*. London: Penguin, 2009. ISBN 9780141192024. (Features commentary on the poetry of Lynette Roberts).

Childe Roland

Jenkins, Nigel. Childe Roland to Welsh Obscurity Came. *Planet: The Welsh Internationalist* 195 (Summer 2009) 86-98. ISSN 00484288.

Henry M. Stanley

Hendon, Steve. Civilizing the Natives: Henry M. Stanley's and Joseph Conrad's Narratives of Identity. *Almanac – Yearbook of Welsh Writing in English: Critical Essays* 14 (2009-10) 1-35.

Dylan Thomas

Annwn, David. Opening the Ellipse: Dylan Thomas and a Maya Deren in America. *Poetry Wales* 44/3 (Winter 2008/2009) 17-18. ISSN 03322202.

Belshaw, P. E. B. On the Edge: a selection of short prose fiction by Patrick Belshaw; and *Once below a time*: a research study of the early short prose fiction of Dylan Thomas. PhD thesis, Newcastle University. BL 493087. 58-13976.

Brown, Terence. The Irish Dylan Thomas: versions and influences. *Irish Studies Review* 7/1 (2009) 45-54.

Riley, Peter. Thomas and Apocalypse. *Poetry Wales* 44/3 (Winter 2008/2009) 12-16. ISSN 03322202.

Thunecke, Jörg. 'Love the words, love the words': Erich Frieds Nachdichtung von Dylan Thomas' U*nder Milk Wood. Neulektüren – New Readings*. Gerhard P. Knapp (editor). Amsterdam, Netherlands: Rodopi, 2009. pp.195-231. ISBN 9042025247.

Edward Thomas

Kendall, Judy. A Genuine Contender. *New Welsh Review* 83 (Spring 2009) 25-32. ISSN 09542116. (Review-article on *The Annotated Collected Poems of Edward Thomas*, edited by Edna Longley (Bloodaxe, 2008), and *Branch-Lines: Edward Thomas and Contemporary Poetry*, edited by Lucy Newlyn and Guy Cuthbertson and published by Enitharmon in 2007).

Seeber, Hans Ulrich. Organic and Textual Circularity in Poems by Edward Thomas and W. H. Auden. *Symbolism: An International Annual Critical Aesthetics* 9 (2009) 129-

140. ISSN 15283623.

Wisniewski, Jacek. *Edward Thomas: A Mirror of England*. Newcastle upon Tyne: Cambridge Scholars Press, 2009. ISBN 1443802107.

R. S. Thomas

Adams, Sam. Letter from Wales. *PN Review* 36/2 (Nov/Dec 2009) 7-9. ISSN 01447076. (Considers the nature of R.S. Thomas's letters to Raymond Garlick, published by Gwasg Gomer in 2009)

Walford Davies, Jason (editor). *R. S. Thomas – Letters to Raymond Garlick, 1951-1999*. Llandysul: Gwasg Gomer, 2009. ISBN 97881843238263.

Sarah Waters

Arias, Rosario. Epilogue: female confinement in Sarah Waters's neo-Victorian fiction. *Stones of Law, Bricks of Shame: Narrating Imprisonment in the Victorian Age*. Jan Alber and Frank Lauterbach (editors). Toronto; Buffalo NY; London: Toronto University Press, 2009. pp. 256-277. ISBN 978-0802098979.

Armitt, Lucie. Garden Paths and Blind Spots. *New Welsh Review* 85 (Autumn 2009) 28-35. ISSN 09542116. (Review-article on Sarah Waters's novel *The Little Stranger*, published by Virago Press in 2009).

Wieckowska, Katarzyna. Dis/Locations: Images of London in Sarah Waters' Fiction. *Images of the City*. Agnieszka Rasmus and Magdelena Cieslak (editors). Newcastle upon Tyne: Cambridge Scholars Press, 2009. pp. 204-215. ISBN 978144380452.

Vernon Watkins

Edwards, Gwynne. Vernon Watkins, Dylan Thomas and the Poetry of Lorca. *Almanac – Yearbook of Welsh Writing in English: Critical Essays* 14 (2009-10) 154-178

Powell Ward, John. Exact Mystery: Some Aspects of Vernon Watkins's Poetics. *Almanac – Yearbook of Welsh Writing in English: Critical Essays* 14 (2009-10) 121-153

Emlyn Williams

Williams, Daniel G. Green in Black. *New Welsh Review* 85 (Autumn 2009) 42-51. ISSN 09542116. On the significance of Emlyn Williams's 1938 play, *The Corn is Green*, in African American culture.

Jane Williams (Ysgafell)

Tyson Roberts, Gwyneth. 'Winding Silkworms' cocoons without a reel: Betsy Cadwaladyr, Jane Williams (Ysgafell) and the Writing of the Autobiography of Elizabeth Davis. *Almanac – Yearbook of Welsh Writing in English: Critical Essays* 14 (2009-10) 36-61.

Raymond Williams

Smith, Dai, Ned Thomas and Daniel G. Williams. The Exchange. *Planet: The Welsh Internationalist* 195 (Summer 2009) 45-66. ISSN 00484288. (An exchange of views on the relevance of Raymond Williams's work today).

Omissions from 2008 bibliography

INDIVIDUAL AUTHORS

David Jones

Black, K. L. 'Those been the cokes wordes and not myne': medieval influences on the structure of David Jones' *The Anathémata*. PhD thesis, London Goldsmiths University. BL 497840. 58-14624.

Leslie Norris

Prothero, James. Leslie Norris and Exile. *Rocky Mountain Review* 62/1 (2008) 45-48. ISSN 03611299.